FAMILY SUPPORT FOR SOCIAL CARE PRACTITIONERS

FAMILY SUPPORT FOR SOCIAL CARE PRACTITIONERS

MARY SHANNON

BLOOMSBURY ACADEMIC
LONDON • NEW YORK • OXFORD • NEW DELHI • SYDNEY

BLOOMSBURY ACADEMIC
Bloomsbury Publishing Plc
50 Bedford Square, London, WC1B 3DP, UK
1385 Broadway, New York, NY 10018, USA
29 Earlsfort Terrace, Dublin 2, Ireland

BLOOMSBURY, BLOOMSBURY ACADEMIC and the Diana logo are trademarks of
Bloomsbury Publishing Plc

First published in Great Britain 2019 by Red Globe Press
Reprinted by Bloomsbury Academic 2022

A catalogue record for this book is available from the British Library.

A catalog record for this book is available from the Library of Congress.

ISBN: PB: 978-1-137-60488-0

To find out more about our authors and books visit www.bloomsbury.com and sign up for
our newsletters.

CONTENTS

PREFACE

The theory and practice of family support has grown in recent years, with the welcome publication of a number of texts and articles from leading writers. It has developed as a policy approach to services and also emerged as an area of study in its own right. It is hoped that this text can add a small contribution, complementing other books, in providing a summary of family support theory and practices that is accessible to students and practitioners of various disciplines. The context across a range of work with vulnerable individuals and with families is included. In focussing on family support as a widely used and applied model, it will explore the key issues and tensions, particularly from a broader policy agenda to improve outcomes.

The book will include some highlighted research in each chapter, which along with the recommended further reading provides pointers for exploration of different topics and the wider relevant literature. There are sections throughout that provide international examples of studies or practice from different countries, suggesting the breadth of application of the ideas. Much of the material does reference the UK context, although within this, notes on the individual countries of Wales, Scotland, Northern Ireland and sometimes Ireland are incorporated. Key tensions or issues are highlighted to promote discussion and reflection. The international and practice examples are intended to provide practical and wider application throughout the text.

The Chapters

Part 1 provides an overview and sets out the main features and aims for the book in Chapter 1, explaining its basis as an approach. Chapters 2 and 3 then move on to explore the contextual background in terms of the historical perspective, the policy framework and the core theoretical underpinnings. Increasingly, practitioners from a multi-agency arena are involved with more complicated and interlinked individuals and families. Developing an understanding and skills in building relationships, undertaking direct work and focussing on strengths reflects this emphasis in working with families.

Part 2 defines and explores groups of service users in family support work. Of importance in this area is the balance of risk, vulnerability, strengths and resilience. Separated into children & families and adults, the two chapters provide some depth on approaches applied to different groups. There are a number of contemporary challenges in supporting and safeguarding vulnerable groups. In both the child and adult field: difficulties in multi-agency working persist, along with the issues of engagement and relationship building with complex service users. Crucially, the tension of balancing support and protection along with ensuring robust outcomes is a feature of current services. Issues in relation to adults' services are outlined with respect to some different areas of interventions, analysing their ethos and application. Although this part of the children's arena often has a lower profile than child protection work, it is covered as an important area of work with children as it is often the largest part of work undertaken.

Part 3 examines the importance of engaging with diversity and the focus on inter-professional working, each of which provide challenges to practitioners. In Chapter 6, issues and practice links are explored in relation to diversity: the significance of this area in terms of the complexity in understanding and engaging with service users from a variety of backgrounds is explored. The theoretical background and methods of multi-agency working are explored in Chapter 7. Some of the difficulties and models of good practice are identified and the reader encouraged to consider these in the light of their own experiences. The overall aim of multi-agency work in enhancing services for both children and adults is covered.

The concluding chapters of Part 4 look to the future, considering contemporary interventions (Chapter 8) and finally drawing together some current themes in the area in Chapter 9. In a developing policy arena, the consideration of future developments is important in maintaining currency in the area. This concluding chapter is an opportunity to draw together some of the dominant current themes in the field.

Aims

The book aims to cover areas of practical skill and knowledge, underpinning theory and critical thinking. Some threads running through the book include: the links between theory and practice; a child and family focus and a person-centered emphasis; links to core values of an anti-oppressive approach and social justice; underlying policy framework; reference to the research base; and finally, discussing the key tensions inherent in a family support approach. The chapters contain a number of features that encourage the reader to engage with research and apply the ideas:

➢ An overview of the content

➢ Practice focus/points for both academic and practice learning

➢ Key points – highlighted

➢ Messages from research

➢ International examples

➢ Further reading suggested

The theoretical basis and the practice principles of the approach are arguably relevant to a range of professions and settings. There is a growing interest across many countries in these ideas, as a set of methods that have key links with the social work and social care tradition. The main aim of this text is to provide a foundation, overview and analysis of 'family support' with service users. Hopefully it can contribute to a focus on a purposeful and well-informed, supportive approach to engaging and intervening with service users.

PART 1

Overview and Context

1

Introduction

Family Support as a practice and theoretical orientation has evolved into a robust set of ideas, with its key applications explored by a number of leading writers and recent texts in the field. The aim of this book is an attempt to cover areas of practical skill and underpinning knowledge that can be useful to a range of relevant practitioners and students. The core theme is that family support *in itself* is of value for a range of practitioners and services. Although subject to policy shifts, it has carved out some clear foundations in theory and practice. Whilst it cannot be seen as a panacea and is subject to the agendas of government, it has potential to be applied across the spectrum of services. At a time when policy in areas such as early intervention, prevention and support are widespread but also facing uncertainty, there are debates that are useful to reflect on. Some of the current tensions centre around support versus intervention, the shift in focus away from wider environmental factors to individual responsibility, and the move from universal to more targeted provision in the general welfare context.

The development of 'family support' can be seen as an attempt to enhance the approach to child welfare, family functioning and services to adults through the life course. In summarising the overall lens that it provides for working with service users in general, definitions will be included here and this will lead on to some of the main initial areas. This introductory chapter will cover:

➢ Definitions of family support

➢ The idea of family support as an approach and a style of working

➢ Inequality, poverty and social justice

➢ Family support as a developing ethos

➢ The formal and informal

➢ Key themes of the book

➢ *Key tension for reflection: Defining a disparate set of practices and ideas*

Definitions of family support

Family support has emerged as a distinct area of theory and practice being defined as '...both a style of work and a set of activities... ' (Dolan et al. 2006: 16). Dolan et al. (2006) furthered this with their outline of 10 principles that characterise the field. It is now generally recognised as a more developed set of ideas (Frost et al., 2015). Family support can be conceptualised as an overall approach: the main theoretical ideas include social support theory, resilience and the overarching theory of the ecological systems framework. Generally, it is an orientation that seeks to work in partnership with families and to empower and strengthen. In this sense it has much in common with underlying values of working with a strengths-based perspective, relationship-based styles and empowerment.

From the literature we see that social support can be categorised into four 'types' of support, namely emotional, concrete (or tangible), advice support and esteem support (Dolan et al., 2006). The provision of emotional support can be found in terms of befriending, mentoring, counselling or listening roles or linking in with therapeutic services. Esteem support is the empowering side of family support, designed to build up the long-term emotional resources of an individual or family. Practical or concrete support, which can include the provision of goods, finances, transport and childcare, is a staple of many services. Finally, there is advice support which could be around parenting, routines or lifestyle choices. Research has shown that families most value the esteem and practical support provided for them, whereas statutory services in particular have traditionally supplied little of this and tended to focus more on advice support (McKeown, 2003). One example of this is the provision of parenting courses (based on advice) for parents following child protection meetings: of course these programmes are of great use, but families' perceptions suggest that some accompanying practical support would add to their effectiveness rather than being seen as the main or only source of support.

Family support in the form of service provision can be part of universally available supportive services that are open to the general population, such as health visiting for infants and young children or other health services. More targeted services are aimed at those families and children who are deemed to be vulnerable or at risk. Services can take a wide variety of forms from centre based (children's centres), home based such as the volunteer visiting schemes Homestart (see https://www.home-start.org.uk/about-us), in schools, through the voluntary sector or a range of ancillary services in both children and adult services. Some more intense services are also home based and involve a key worker visiting: in the case of a family with children, this may consist of several hours per day, often at particular times which may be early morning or out of hours, that reflects the families' need around bedtime or morning routines.

In many ways the development of family support services is seen as a success story. Providing various types of support that people need appears to promote progress with often entrenched issues. This is shown in the evaluation of outcomes from various interventions, as the overview by Frost et al. (2015) details. In the children and families arena it has been particularly useful as a way of focussing on outcomes for both the child and the family. User reports of such services are generally positive with reports of high levels of engagement.

Key point

The rise of family support ideas in the policy arena has ensured that the concept has become a central pillar in the provision of services. It has moved from an 'add on' or an optional extra to being a substantial part of our thinking in many areas of service provision.

The idea of family support as an approach and a style of working

The theoretical underpinnings suggest that its application across services as an ethos and way of working is now a key element of provision. At government levels, the methods are gaining increasing prominence, both in the well-developed sector in leading economies and the emerging sector in other countries, although often in the current context of retrenched resources. Whilst family support as a preventative strategy and a focus on early intervention has emerged, statutory services themselves in many jurisdictions have become narrower in their remit.

At a service level, we know that strengths-based styles of working are really valued by service users. These elements are increasingly seen to be fundamental to the success of many interventions, adding to arguments that the perspectives can be of value across the range of services. The role of workers and those who provide such support in a variety of different settings and roles can be seen as crucial.

Inequality, poverty and social justice

Support to individuals, families and communities is set in the context of rising inequality and poverty levels in the UK and beyond. As an example, in Birmingham, England's second largest city, there are estimates that up to 100,000 children are living in poverty, and that there is a difference of over 10 years' life expectancy and nearly double unemployment rates between the most affluent and most deprived areas (Birmingham Poverty Truth Commission). An understanding of this structural context is crucial for the family support sector and also an appreciation of the impact on daily lives. The Poverty Truth Commission began in Scotland in 2009 and now features across a number of UK cities. It focusses on firstly hearing the stories of those living in poverty, recognising that this is not a homogenous group; then the organisation works on creating key alliances to influence policy makers and services locally. The narratives can be powerful, and also it can be empowering for those involved to have their stories heard. Similarly, exploring the effects of poverty on children shows that personal and psychological effects related to shame and stress, and attempts to cover these up, are key features of children's lives, along with limited social opportunities and deprivation of basic items such as food and clothing (Ridge, 2011).

This context of widening inequality is exacerbated by the landscape of service provision, with ongoing patterns of reductions in state-funded provision across all sectors, a paring down of wider supports and reductions in welfare provision. In terms of the position and future possibilities for family support, these issues are central.

Key point

Inequality, poverty and social justice.

A family support orientation takes a wider ecological perspective (outlined in Chapter 3), encouraging a focus on the effects of material disadvantage and inequality. This is well linked with arguments for both social justice and greater equality for the often disadvantaged service user groups that practitioners are engaged with.

> ### *Messages from research/International perspective*
>
> It can be suggested that the application of family support as a way of working and with the principles of a strengths base in itself is of value, which is a main theme of the book. Research has shown the importance of process factors in service provision: a crucial part of this can be the style adopted by practitioners. Often methods of working with a distinctly strengths-based slant are evident, even within poorly funded settings.
>
> The discussion of these concepts is relevant across different jurisdictions as statutory interventions become increasingly located at the remedial rather than the preventative end of services. The fundamental principles can be valuable across all services, and writers in the field have been instrumental in raising the profile of family support practices and ways of working.
>
> Taking an international perceptive, an analysis by Daly et al. (2015) looked at family and parenting support in 33 different countries. It is useful to consider and compare how the ideas are integrated in a variety of social and economic contexts. This is an insightful resource in terms of providing a snapshot and comparing how the methods have been applied in different ways internationally.
>
> The report is available at the following link: https://www.unicef-irc.org/publications/pdf/01family_support_layout_web.pdf.

Family support as a developing ethos

The theoretical basis and the principles are relevant to a range of professions and settings. There is an increased interest internationally in these ideas, particularly given the emphasis on social investment (which will be discussed in Chapter 2 of the book). Family Support has moved on from being a 'warm and fuzzy' (Dolan et al., 2006: 11) concept to a more robust set of practices that have links with the social work and social care tradition. With a focus on multi-agency, relational and strengths-based working, this chimes with many of the recommendations of the Munro Review (2011) in the UK. Here, the need for a high level of skill and a clear knowledge base around relationships, undertaking direct work and an emphasis on balancing strengths and risk, has been highlighted, and signalled a new slant in social work and wider areas with children and families. Therefore it is timely to concentrate on a *purposeful* and *well-informed* supportive approach to engaging and intervening with service users.

As a key form of intervention, it has become established at a policy level in many countries. This is particularly in the early intervention and preventative arena. Additionally, the increased working between health and social care has necessitated more holistic thinking on a range of issues. The core values that underpin this are being clearly person and family centred in the wider context of holistic and multi-agency working in this arena. There are a number of contemporary challenges in supporting and safeguarding vulnerable groups that can be discussed: for much of the book, there will be examples from family work, with some reference to wider adult services along with a specific chapter on some adult provision.

Key point

In both the adult and child fields, difficulties in multi-agency working persist, along with the issues of engagement and relationship building with complex service users. Crucially, the tension of balancing support and protection along with ensuring robust outcomes are important features of current practice.

The formal and informal

Whilst a good deal of the focus of this book will be on practitioners who provide or facilitate support, the emphasis will be on both formal and informal areas. Formal support can be described as compensatory, where services intervene to provide one or more of the four types of support: this being provided to fill a gap or bolster what an individual or family has, in order to resolve or alleviate problems. However, it is widely recognised from the literature that the principle source of support for most people lies in the informal help which is gained from family, close relationships, wider friends and family and universal welfare provision. The goal of much intervention is to strengthen, build or expand on this to ensure its durability as it is the preferred option of families (Dunst, 2008). Additionally, we must consider that formal services can often be perceived to be stigmatising by families (Ghate and Hazel, 2002). Approaches that seek to expand natural networks and positive help-seeking behaviour may be more developmental (Connolly, 2017) and sustainable in the longer term.

Practice focus

The Social Provision Scale (Social Network Questionnaire, Adolescent Specific Version) is a tool that identifies types of support by source. The tool was adapted by Dolan (2006) for use with adolescents.

This was designed to provide an overall score of support available to young people, but also to elicit information relating to social support. An example of this applied is its use with unaccompanied minors – this group of young people may typically have lower levels of informal help (from family or friends) and therefore increased levels of formal support can be tailored to their needs.

Kali is a 15-year-old female who had arrived in the UK 8 months ago as an unaccompanied minor and has been placed to live with foster carers. Leaving behind her brother and other family members, she has made some friends, is supported by a project worker, has been attending a group after school and has a new pet (see Jack and Donnellan, 2013 on the role that pets can play for young people). Turning to the idea of using a tool or questionnaire to explore social networks, consider what networks Kali would consider that she has and which would be important to her. In order to facilitate Kali in filling out the questionnaire, you would have taken a sensitive approach; considering that she may feel she has lost many of her social networks, the aim would be to build on what can help her going forward.

Spotlight on reflective practice

Reflective practice is at the core of family support (Dolan et al., 2006) essentially, so that practitioners and managers at all levels maintain a clear perspective on the processes that impact on individuals and families.

The cycle of reflection has been well outlined by key writers such as Schon's classic model of 'reflection – on action' and 'reflection – in action'; or Kolb's cycle, where the practitioner moves from an active participant in a concrete experience to reflecting on it, analysing what happened and what could have been done differently, to the implementation of a new idea (in Thompson, 2006).

Features of reflection are (adapted from Brown and Rutter, 2008):

- Awareness of all aspects of a situation – feelings and thoughts
- Explore and link to relevant literature – challenge and question underlying assumptions
- Evaluate – how well? What about?
- Learning – produce new understanding or solutions

▶

◀

Reflection has a clear tradition in social work and other professions: it has the potential to bring practical experiences and theoretical perspectives together so that action in often chaotic or complex circumstances can be deconstructed and lead to changing approaches (Adams in Tovey, 2007). Critical reflection has the principle of both challenging underlying assumptions that lie behind our actions and actively seeking to influence the future, with a more in-depth exploration.

These processes in busy, complex and varied services remain crucial to the family support ethos and the emphasis on the experiences of individuals, children and families.

Key point

In focussing on family support as a widely used and applied model, we can see it as part of the wider agenda to improve outcomes. The issues and tensions, particularly from a policy perspective, provide the context across the whole range of work with vulnerable individuals and with families.

Key tension for reflection: Defining a disparate set of practices and ideas

Family support itself has evolved in the way it is perceived; to become a well-defined area in the policy and practice arena. Writers such as Dolan et al. (2006) and Frost et al. (2015) outline some of the trajectory of this movement. From examples of projects that provide quite universal and lower levels of input to the more intensive projects for families in greater need, the notion now takes a central place in current provision in many countries.

This was evident in the UK in the services that the flagship Sure Start centres provided for families: these were a key feature of the then Labour government's agenda. In another example, for Wales the Families First programme forms part of an overall and developed strategy that views provision of universal services alongside targeted inputs as part of the wider anti-poverty strategy.

What has worked well is the pulling together of theoretical tenets and principles that characterise a supportive perspective across all these different domains and jurisdictions. It remains a challenge, however, to tie these different service elements and various modes of operation together into a coherent body of ideas, given that the term 'family support' has more prominence in some countries. The work that has distilled practice into core messages continues and has proved useful, with a focus on how family support manifests in practice being key (Devaney and Dolan, 2017). Arguably to demonstrate its value and secure funding, family support needs the development to continue, as advocated by others (Frost et al., 2015; Canavan et al., 2016). The recent 'Action for Children' report (2013) highlights that there have been severe reductions across the UK in services for young people in particular. This current context makes the area both timely and essential.

Further reading

Daly, M., Bruckhauf, Z., Byrne, J., Pecnik, N., Samms-Vaughan, M., Bray, R. & Margaria, A., 2015. *Family and Parenting Support: Policy and Provision in a Global Context* (No. innins770).
This international report is available at the following link: https://www.uni cef-irc.org/publications/pdf/01family_support_layout_web.pdf.

Dolan, P. (2006). Assessment, intervention & self appraisal tools for family support. In Dolan, P., Canavan, J. and Pinkerton, J. (eds), *Family Support as Reflective Practice* (pp. 197–210). London: Jessica Kingsley.
This chapter in a text on family support focusses on practice applications of family support including the Social Provision Scale.

Early Intervention Foundation website. Available at: http://www.eif.org.uk/.

The Early Intervention Foundation (EIF) is a charity and one of the Government's What Works Centres.

Frost, N., Abbott, S. and Race, T., 2015. *Family Support: Prevention, Early Intervention and Early Help* (Introduction: pp.1–6). Cambridge: John Wiley & Sons.
A comprehensive policy and practice guide to family support.

Glass, N., 1999. Sure start: the development of an early intervention programme for young children in the United Kingdom. *Children & Society, 13*(4), pp. 257–264.
This early publication is useful in considering a key application of early intervention in the UK.

2

Setting the Context: A Historical and Policy Perspective

In setting out the overall context of family support, this chapter will firstly provide a brief history of the philanthropic roots of family support, through to recent decades where its key place in provision will be outlined. Linking this to policy, the aim is to explore how the practices and ideas of family support have both persisted and evolved.

There will be an analysis of the development of the whole notion of family support as a both a remedial and an early intervention/preventative approach. Some of the main tensions and issues here, including the balancing of support and intervention, are explored and will be returned to in subsequent chapters. The issue of the evidence-informed practice movement and the focus on outcomes that has resulted will be critically examined: this has been a particular feature of services in the current climate.

An overview of the content:

➢ The historical development of family support

➢ The general policy agenda and family support

➢ The preventative and early intervention agenda

➢ Early intervention: the early years and families

➢ The issue of evidence-informed practice and the 'outcomes' agenda

➢ *Key tension for reflection: Support or intervention*

The historical development of family support

Earlier in the twentieth century, the McMillan sisters in England and Grace and Edith Abbot in America are recognised as carrying out pioneering work supporting poor and disadvantaged children and families

(Costin,1983; Giardiello, 2013). It seems the developing industrialisation and rapidly changing society resulting in migration to cities produced levels of need, poverty and poor health particularly among families. In exploring a history of the poor or problem family, Welshman (1999) cites the concern shown by philanthropic middle-class 'visitors' providing practical and emotional help. Burnham (2016) writes about this in his exploration of the history of social work and social services: the tradition of home visiting by charity workers to mainly poor families formed the origins of social work, centred around the home visit and intervening with families in their home environment (Ferguson, 2011).

From a child welfare perspective in particular, issues began to come to the forefront of public policy. At this time, there were movements from a public health perspective to improve the rates of child mortality, with living conditions, widespread poverty, poor nutrition levels, and lack of sanitation and medical care resulting in widespread disease and ill-health, particularly amongst young children in urban areas. Such developments were often predicated by the disintegration of community structures that catered for the vulnerable in rapidly growing populations, with the idea of the state taking responsibility for some family and community issues (Holman, 1988). So, family support as a practice orientation has a long history and interestingly some similarities with its earlier roots. The core elements can be seen in both the past and present: providing tangible inputs to some extent and with some family-based elements to meet need.

Key point

The interesting aspect of taking a historical perspective shows how similar the fundamental elements of family support are across time. Writing about a project for families in Norwich in the 1940s, Taylor and Rogaly (2007) talk about workers encountering families with multiple and enduring problems with health, finances, living conditions and 'household management' issues. In describing the kind of intensive practical and emotional input to 'chaotic' families, the project bears much resemblance to more current intensive approaches that attempt to tackle very similar issues with families.

The general policy agenda and family support

Family support has become more important in policy terms in many countries. The development of more widespread welfare in western countries in the last century led to an approach of providing for the needs of citizens, with the development of policies around the 'big five' areas of income maintenance, payments, housing, health and social services, and education (Baldock et al., 2011). This had centred to some extent on provision at a universal level where services are available to all, but increasingly the focus was on more vulnerable populations. In recent decades neoliberal economies have seen a move from welfare state to market-based approaches, with an emphasis on responsibility rather than rights, the marketisation of services and more conditional welfare benefits (Hudson and Lowe, 2009). The general pattern is for a more limited state role in provision that sees citizens as consumers and government taking on more of a regulatory function (Alcock et al., 2014). With this residual role of the welfare state, there have been cutbacks in service provision and a narrowing to risk management of vulnerable citizens.

A shift from universal services that takes a more developmental and preventative approach to a more limited safety net and directed approach is evident (Green and Clarke, 2016). The current retrenchment experienced to some extent in all countries as a result of austerity policies (Bonoli et al., 2000) has added a complexity to welfare provision. With the requirements for more cost-effective and streamlined delivery, services have often become more targeted.

Where family support fits into this welfare landscape is contested and is an area where definition is required to forefront and make explicit its role (Canavan et al., 2016). It can form a key pillar of practice and policy such as Sure Start in the UK, or if it is seen as an add-on can easily become part of a restrictive and shrinking provision.

Writing in 1997 Parton had argued that a key issue was '...how policies and practice in relation to child protection integrate with and are supported by policies and practices that are concerned with family support and child welfare more generally' (p. 1). Gibbons (1990: 15) had described family support in particular as '....a special type of social support'. One example of family support through this period are family centres which, starting out in the 1970s with a largely local and non-stigmatising approach, showed a changing and adaptable role, many incorporating children's centres/childcare in response to policy priorities (Tunstill et al., 2006). Parton (2005: 82) notes that policy shifted in the 1990s with a change of government attempting to ambitiously go '...beyond simply rebalancing family support and child protection, to embrace concerns about parenting, early intervention, supporting the family and regenerating the community more generally'. Basically, the role of the state became broader and a new interest in childhood was signalled. It has been suggested that this state interest has in fact resulted in increased and unnecessary levels of surveillance of poorer families (Garrett, 2004), and there are more recent calls for a wider public health approach to child protection that goes beyond a multi-agency risk assessment-based model (Barlow and Callam, 2011).

The rise of family support in the UK: A policy example

There had been a general move towards family supportive services at both universal and targeted levels over the last decade or so in England. In the children's arena, the introduction of the Common Assessment Framework (CAF) in England and Wales was part of the expanding of safeguarding responsibilities: these initiatives indicated a specific policy slant. The original Laming report (2003) and the subsequent policy and legislation in the form of the Every Child Matters policy and the Children Act 2004 had mandated this broadening of timely assistance to children and families.

This approach incorporated two aspects.

Firstly, the aim was to *widen* the remit to support families and identify child welfare concerns. This can be seen in the use of the term 'safeguarding' and the emphasis on a range of professionals having responsibility. Secondly, it was aimed at providing help *earlier* to families, before the threshold for referral to children's social care arose, as seen in the CAF. Generally, there had been a movement to recognise the benefits of providing both broader and more directed inputs.

In Wales, a more comprehensive family support policy programme has been devised, particularly aimed at disadvantaged and poor families, that is ambitious in its remit and incorporates several strands, as part of the Building a Brighter Future: Early Years and Childcare Plan, launched in 2013 (Pithouse and Jones, 2015). In Scotland, the GIRFEC policy guidance which places early intervention and a holistic view of child welfare at the centre has become a key driver for the system (Rose, 2015). These different directions are interesting, as compared to the relegation of the 'Every Child Matters' agenda in the UK.

The preventative and early intervention agenda

In order to understand developments in policy, a number of models have sought to map out the different policy approaches to citizens and to families. Loraine Fox-Harding's model (1991) set out four orientations in relation to state policy and families:

➢ The private arena of the family that is largely off-limits to state intervention in the 'laissez-faire' model;

➢ The paternalistic state concerned with protection;

➤ The birth-family orientated; and

➤ Children's rights

These provide a useful framework to examine the law and policy of a country because they address the ideas or values that are behind policies. Elements of each probably can be seen in most legislation but there is likely to be an emphasis on one or more aspects, such as the child centred/protection slant in England currently (see Featherstone et al., 2014).

Using another lens, the welfare regimes outlined by Esping-Anderson (1990) is a model that has been widely used and adapted to consider the different social policy approaches that countries take. With a consideration of the amount of state expenditure and how it is distributed enabling him to broadly categorise their underpinning ideas, this model describes:

➤ The liberal regime – a more 'hands-off' or residual tendency to general welfare;

➤ The conservative model with some state intervention, but targeted provision; and

➤ The higher investment slant typical of Nordic countries set within a generous welfare regime.

Considering the features of various approaches in different countries and over time using these models can be useful showing the overall approach. More recently, though, in many countries there is an increasing state involvement in families that characterises what has become widely referred to as the 'social investment' thinking of many jurisdictions today (see Featherstone, 2005). This term refers to government policies aimed at promoting strengths, capabilities and opportunity for people: the goal of providing modest amounts of funding to gain a return in the future in terms of individuals' increased skill, potential and employability. As Gray (2013) points out, in many countries the liberal/ neoliberal ideas of residual state spending and provision have been softened with these social investment policies and the remit of providing carefully targeted services.

Looking at early intervention and prevention, both have been characteristic of policy response in many countries. The terms refer to both earlier in the life course, which includes the early years, and also early in the problem. Although discussion has largely been about the early years, as outlined below, in fact early input and prevention can be seen at all stages of the lifecourse such as the growing concern with more preventative and community-based health and social care services for older people (this is an area that will be mentioned in Chapter 5). Prevention has in some cases been seen as preventing future and more costly outcomes, family support provision that aims to prevent children coming into the care system. Despite the growing interest, though, it is often not easy to argue for prevention given that it is harder to prove its success in the short term (Gibbons, 1990).

Early intervention: The early years and families

The ideas of early support and prevention have become popular in policy terms in many countries. Within different countries in Europe, labour activation policies seek to incentivise as many individuals as possible to undertake paid work: We saw this in the UK as the focus of welfare policy shifted to these aims (see Lister, 2004; Featherstone, 2005). The activation of females into the labour force does involve a consideration of the care of young children (through childcare) and an interest in the structure and function of family life. Holt (2011) also sees the growth in policy terms of 'parental determinism' whereby parents are seen as the prime influence on future anti-social behaviour, social inclusion and social mobility. The emphasis on producing more independent, economically active citizens in the future can mean childhood is viewed as a key period, and creates a political interest in parenting itself (Churchill, 2011; Leverett, 2014) Providing support to enable people to carry out parenting roles and increase their skills is a narrower and more specific focus than family support more generally (Miller, 2010).

This interest in family and children was seen in the child-centred strategy developed by the leading European policy expert Gosta Esping-Anderson in 2008. It is mirrored at a more global scale, with a renewed emphasis on family as a site of policy implementation across many countries (Murray and Barnes, 2010). The World Bank, for example, promotes the concept of investing in children in poorer countries (Engle et al., 2007), and we have seen a focus on promoting childcare provision in wealthier countries, encouraging workforce activity across the genders, and more generally a prioritisation of resources in the early years.

Key point

The spotlight on families and on the period of childhood as a time when social investment can be implemented has increased. The famous Perry Highscope project longitudinal study in America had showed a financial return for the state with every dollar put into the early years (see Schweinhart, 2005): this has become a much quoted study.

▶

◀

One particular aspect of this shift of resources to young children has been the growth of evidence around neuroscience. Wastell and White (2017) have recently written with concern about this growing interest in the effects on young children's growth and development. The benefits of investing in the early years has led to discussion about the importance of the under fives and the need for resources here. Whilst the early years are of course an important time, some argue that the claims do not take sufficient account of the role of environmental factors and the key concept of resilience that can ensure later development and recovery for children also.

In terms of families and children, governments have always been interested in families to some extent and seen them as a concern of policy, varying through historical periods. Parton (2014) traces this development and charts the course in the UK over the last four decades providing a history of 'governing the family'. Generally, we can see that intervening in families has become an increasing concern for governments. In common with many other European countries, the approach to what have become known as 'troubled' or multi-problem families and the response to social problems in general, including poverty and social exclusion, has risen to the forefront in terms of policy imperatives. However it is very debatable whether this focal point is at all positive (Foley, 2011). A less visible aspect is that multiple and cumulative social exclusion can disproportionately affect different groups along lines of gender, ethnicity or disability (Adams, 2011).

From this policy perspective, children, young people and adolescents are seen as resources for society in the future and there is a drive to invest early in their development. These ideas were very much taken on board by New Labour in the UK, which saw the development of government intervention into some families' lives at an unprecedented level. Others have been critical of this approach in terms of a lack of consideration of children and their rights as they are seen as future resources for society (Featherstone, 2014). The sociology of childhood is important here – being a perspective that sees the value of childhood itself and the present (Mayall, 2015) rather than the idea of children as 'becoming' for the future.

International example

An example from the international arena can be found in the overview of family support policy in Eastern Europe over the last two decades (Rostgaard, 2004). In many Eastern European countries there was a short transition from almost wholly state-run

▶

◄

services to economies driven much more by market and labour market forces. Initially this led to an increase in universal provision for families in many cases, but with cost pressures on service provision, this tended to move more quickly to more restricted approaches.

The emphasis has tended to be on cash benefits for families with young children, rather than on concrete services. Some argue that this can leave gaps in services like the provision of early years childcare or practical family help. As Rostgaard points out, the provision is certainly welcomed but does not take a holistic approach to child welfare and family functioning.

The development of the use of family support at a policy level is global, but there is still variation in different countries, with policy reflecting the local intersection of political, social and economic factors.

Practice focus

It may be useful at this point to consider a practice application of recent policy in the area of supporting families. The primary aim of FIP (Family Intervention Projects) services as intense provision for 'hard to reach' families through a key worker system.

The main feature of the model was a clear approach based on research about what can work with families. The FIP model was based on a project, known as the Dundee project, run in Scotland by Action for Children. FIPs generally responded to very challenging families who had usually been known to a number of services for some time, often with limited engagement or success. The FIP workers typically spent between 8 and 15 hours per week with families, carrying out a variety of practical, therapeutic and developmental tasks. The provision was planned following an initial assessment and reviewed regularly. Involvement of a range of agencies to meet the needs of the family or children is another feature of the model. This multi-agency approach ensuring that for at least a period of time there is a coordinated team around these families.

Although many FIP projects have since transformed into the Troubled Families projects, many of the features of the model remain and this type of intensive service retains its importance (Jones et al., 2015).

A case was referred to FIP because of concerns about neglect, a chaotic household and parents not coping. Georgina had been physically abused and neglected as a child. She had two children with her partner Dave, who she met when she was 17, but there was domestic abuse so she left and met Tom: they have had another six children together. Georgina has been diagnosed with depression; Tom suffers from diabetes. The older children had been previously in care because of neglect.

►

◀

Megan is 16; Kyle, 14, has been getting in trouble locally, was expelled from school and can be aggressive at home; Jasmine is 10; Gary is 8 and has learning difficulties; Lauren is 7 and very attention seeking; Tracey is 5 and very quiet; Rob is 2 and Georgina finds his behaviour difficult; David is the baby.

Considering the four types of support outlined in Chapter 1, what would you consider as possibilities for the family?

The issue of evidence-informed practice and the 'outcomes' agenda

The evidence-based practice movement has strong roots in the US where the emphasis is on quantitative research and randomised controlled trials (RCTs), where as European evaluative traditions are rooted more in the qualitative tradition. Whilst there are certainly critiques of evidence-based or evidence-informed practice, it has brought many benefits to the field in terms of an emphasis on outcomes for service users (McLaughlin, 2011). The phrase the 'what works agenda' has been coined to represent this renewed focus on outcomes. In the UK this had been seen clearly in the Allen review (2011) which set out services that should be funded based on the existence of an RCT as part of the evidence base. The recent development of the What Works Centre for England and Wales will be interesting as it develops, with a clear government spotlight on particular priorities. The EIF is a charity and one of the Government's What Works Centres, with their website featuring guides to evaluated services and current research (available at: http://www.eif.org.uk/).

Evidence-informed practice, growing in influence, has indicated that a whole raft of provision for families could produce positive results. With the widespread view that some form of early 'help' does make sense, the UK has looked to the US in particular where many services have undergone substantial evaluation. One example is the Family Nurse Partnership programme for vulnerable first-time mothers (see Jack and Donnellan, 2013: 88–89 for a brief overview), based on successful home-based schemes in the US. There has been a growing interest in purposeful input that produces actual outcomes for children, young people and their families. A key aspect of this is a focus on value for money, with services required to produce evidence of such (McAuley et al., 2006). A notable example of this recently in the UK has been the Troubled

Families agenda with its 'payments by results' stipulation for future funding – this has become included in provision contracts in the adult social care sector also.

There has certainly been a general growth of evidence-informed practice in services and a concern about value for money and evidencing outcomes (Edwards et al., 2016). Stevens et al. (2010) in their research review in the 'What works for children' project suggested that looking at the cost effectiveness of interventions isn't always clear in complex social situations and that making a social judgement could usefully be a part of this. As McLaughlin (2011) suggests, social work outcomes are generally not easy to measure due to the inherent complexity of people and their environment. So-called soft, qualitative data can be hugely important, as it often involves actually listening to service users' perspectives (McLeod, 2008). Within the emphasis on outcomes, the quality of relationships and ability to see family strengths remain key to interventions in children's services (Molly et al., 2017). Arguably more emphasis should be placed on the whole process and why programmes are successful:

> We need to move from a concentration on what works, to learning more on why it works. (Frost and Dolan, 2017: 384).

Messages from research

Softer outcomes

With the increased focus on value for money and measurable results, there is often less emphasis on what can be described as 'soft outcomes'. These effects are usually very important to service users, although they are more difficult to pinpoint and measure. In fact, there is the whole issue of who decides what is a good outcome, as shown in the Troubled Families programme in England and the rise of 'payment by results' service contracts. Family support encourages us to look at the service user perspective and to consider the emotional and psychological benefits of services.

Effects such as an increase in self-esteem and self-efficacy are viewed as being difficult to measure as they are 'softer' outcomes. Parr (2016) in her research on intensive projects points out that the relationship-based working as part of key worker skills is producing positive effects for families. From the family perspective, it could be argued that these factors are just as important as the more formal 'outcomes'.

Practice focus

The practice tool known as an 'Outcomes Star' is used and adapted in many ser-vices. The tool enables services and users to capture progress across a number of domains. In mental health settings, using a recovery model, domains including health, living skills, employment and relationships are used. Importantly, though, softer outcomes such as identity, self-esteem and levels of hope are considered. Details of the tool, which was developed by Family Action, can be found at: http://www.outcomesstar.org.uk/.

Samples of outcome stars and further information are also available at this link.

Consider the example of the family above: on the 'outcome star' where do you think that Georgina and Tom would initially rate the family in the areas of Physical health, Emotional well-being, Keeping your children safe, Social networks, Education and learning, Boundaries and behaviour, Family routine, and Home and money?

Key point: The ideological position of family support

An important point about the principles, theory and practice of family support is that it represents an *ideological position*. Central to this is the idea of it being provided to meet people's needs, as an approach that incorporates a set of principles and that embodies a style of working that is rooted in a strengths-based perspective. At a time when services are being pared down, and targeting of services is increasing, fam-ily support really emphasises a *preventative stance* to needs and problems. In the context of other discourses such as 'child rescue' ideas and the neoliberal value of individual responsibility, the importance of this ideological stance is clear.

Key tension for reflection: Support or intervention

The recent policy approach to supporting families and their children in both the current context in the UK and internationally has shifted to a stronger state role in protective *intervention* (Featherstone et al., 2014). This is coupled with cutbacks of some of the wider prevention and ser-vices in the UK (Action for Children, 2013) and many other countries. Alongside this, the protection and welfare of children and services for families have been widely acknowledged to have become dominated by a risk oriented approach as will be explored further in later chapters.

One area of critique is around the idea of intervention rather than support. This can be seen in some of the intensive FIP projects and more explicitly in the 'Troubled Families' UK agenda where contracts are a feature and the service can be nonvoluntary and stigmatising (Beddoe, 2014). Similarly in the adult services arena, the payment by results criteria for funding of services produces this emphasis on outcomes (Glasby and Tew, 2015) rather than support in itself. The prevalence of issues in disadvantaged communities with high levels of poverty leads to criticism of family support and social work becoming a 'sticking plaster' solution to structural and economic problems (Adams et al., 2009). Many issues of adult, child and family well-being are inescapably linked to wider political and policy issues (Rixon, 2011). Some argue that the whole notion of *support* is being overtaken by *intervention* (Frost et al., 2015), which suggests that family support approaches can usefully try to reclaim this area.

Further reading

http://www.outcomesstar.org.uk/ Website
This provides a practical application and guidance about outcomes for service users and how we might foster these in an empowering way.

Fitzsimons P. & William Teager, W., 2018. *The cost of late intervention in Northern Ireland.*
This report analysing the estimated costs of not intervening earlier is on the Early Intervention Website, available at: http://www.eif.org.uk/.

Parr, S., 2016. Conceptualising 'the relationship' in intensive key worker support as a therapeutic medium. *Journal of Social Work Practice*, 30(1), pp. 25–42.
A useful article that really looks at worker interactions with service users in family support, giving a perspective on policy in this area with more 'troubled families' and how this is enacted in practice.

Parton, N., 2014. *The Politics of Child Protection: Contemporary Developments and Future Directions.* Palgrave Macmillan.
A thorough and interesting contemporary overview is set out in Parton's book.

Rostgaard, T., 2004. Family support policy in central and eastern Europe – A decade and a half of transition. *Early Childhood and Family Policy Series, 8,* pp. 1–37.
As family support develops in different countries and contexts, this article gives a helpful comparative overview.

3

Theoretical Underpinnings

This chapter maps out the solid basis of family support approaches, in terms of being rooted in clear ideas: family support practice is underpinned by a set of related theoretical concepts (Canavan et al., 2016). It has been noted that: '...as a diverse and difficult-to-define concept covering a range of practices, it is unsurprising that family support is underpinned by a number of theoretical approaches' (Frost and Dolan, 2012: 40).

Ideas from family and childhood studies provide a backdrop to the discussions and these will be examined as the key bases in the field. Ecological systems theory is the overarching framework for family support practice, in common with other disciplines. The notion of resilience for both children and their families has become a growing area of interest for services and will be explored as an important application. Social support theory as a core basis for family support is set in its contemporary context along with the ideas of social capital.

The chapter will cover:

➤ Families and children

➤ Social support

➤ Resilience

➤ Ecological systems theory

➤ Social capital

➤ Human development and attachment theories

➤ *Key tension for reflection: The child-centred/family tension in family support*

Families and children

In considering 'family' itself, its changing and contested nature is summarised by many writers in terms of both widely acknowledged changes in family type/structure, along with key debates about the nature and role of family (Smart, 2007). An analysis of family across time and space from different theoretical perspectives shows it is variously described as a social construct, a site of oppression, and a product of patriarchy. Political agendas and moral overtones are tied in with these debates, and family support is necessarily involved in this by its essence and can be shaped by general family policy in a country. Functionalist and more traditional ideas have been criticised for a lack of recognition of family in terms of gender oppression and for their heteronormative basis (Edwards and Gillies, 2012). There has been a focus in literature on the role of the family in the socialisation of children, caring (for children and other family members), as an economic unit, as a source of relationship or as a lifestyle choice.

A summary of changes shows that there are greater numbers of cohabiting couples, separated and blended families, lone-parent households, same-sex families and lower birth rates both in the UK and most western countries (Cunningham and Cunningham, 2014). There are also fewer siblings as family sizes continue to be smaller (Jamieson, 2011). Giddens had presented a perspective that relationships and families had largely become about choice and companionship and although this rang true, it has since been criticised as insufficiently considering class and gender (Featherstone et al., 2014). Also, despite these well-established patterns of change with same-sex relationships, alternative family types and cultural practices, the notion of a normative family is a persistent idea (O'Dell, 2011), reminding us that our mainstream ideas about both childhood and the family are largely a social construction.

The idea of how people actually experience family has emerged as a stream of contemporary thought. Although family in some form has an enduring existence, the variety of family life is acknowledged in policy, with 'families of choice' and 'family practices' emerging as preferred terms in this area (Morgan, 2011). Here, the emphasis is on how people engage with and experience family life in its different forms: essentially quality of relationship rather than family type is seen as important. Family support looks to family in its broadest sense as a potential for support such as the wide network drawn on in a family group conference (see Chapter 4), being cognizant of the caring and cared-for roles within families that overlaps with networks of friendships (Jamieson, 2011). From another angle, we know that family is increasingly the site of intimate partner abuse and domestic abuse (Thompson, 2011), and there is an emerging recognition of child to parent violence (Coogan, 2011). The impact of housing and employment policies is felt perhaps at its sharpest in the family. Complexities to the family sphere are added by household income reductions and a rise of in-work poverty during periods of austerity, which leads to stress. This can also include childcare issues from precarious labour, gender and work balances (Ba, 2017).

In terms of policy, governments do discuss who families are and how policy should approach them (Foley, 2011). Murray and Barnes (in Morris, 2012) suggest that types of family are conceptualised by government as either resourceful, responsible, antisocial or socially excluded families. There is an increased interest in the social construction of parenting, parents' responsibilities and a trend for a greater level of emotional investment in children that will be discussed further in later chapters (Holt, 2011; Featherstone et al., 2014).

Similarly, how society perceives children and their treatment has changed over time. The way we depict childhood has ranged from 'little adults' in past centuries, to periods of industrial development when it was seen as the norm for children to work, often for long hours, leading to philanthropic campaigns to improve children's lives (Wyness, 2012). Our more modern view of childhood as a distinctive phase, to be protected and nurtured, has developed, with issues about both protection and promoting children's potential becoming central in recent times to our thinking (Moss and Petrie, 2005). The sociology of childhood as a theoretical approach has been vital in shaping this – focussing on the child's perspective and on childhood having its own culture and characteristics. Rather than viewing children in society being solely defined and controlled by adults, this perspective acknowledges the active role of children as being individuals with their own rights and autonomy (James and James, 2004).

This development of the children's rights movement has seen rights that are enshrined in law and legislative principles in many countries. They can be difficult to implement meaningfully due to factors such as children's perceived lack of competence on matters that affect them and complex situations (Race and O'Keefe, 2017). Perhaps children's rights have advanced but as adults support or advocate for children's views, this can be a paternalistic approach where children end up being '...passive recipients of adult protection and good will...' (Lansdown, 2011: 143). The rights approach has also largely taken an ethno-centrist approach based on western views and values (Edwards, 2015). However, advancing children's rights has certainly enabled their voices to be heard more, in comparison to historic abuse cases in previous decades where adult versions of events were dominant.

Children's welfare is further complicated as what we consider is best for children continues to change over time, for example, debates on the use of physical chastisement, which many children's advocacy groups heavily criticise from a rights perspective (Davies and Duckett, 2016).

The conceptualisation of childhood has also been mixed in relation to older children and adolescents who have often been seen in popular discourse in quite a negative way. In historical terms, adolescence has relatively recently been recognised as a distinct developmental stage between child and adulthood: there is a very clear social and cultural context to youth as a construction that varies over time and young people are often blamed for societal problems (Bright, 2015). In the youth work tradition, there has been a focus on the particular needs of young people, rather than seeing them as a problem group (Spence, 2007). Recent criticisms that services have failed to listen to adolescents or mistakenly not seen them as vulnerable have been highlighted in the Child Sexual Exploitation reports (Jay, 2014). Through such events, adolescence is being viewed increasingly as a complex period in terms of young people's development with the vulnerability of young people being increasingly acknowledged.

Spotlight on fathers

Fathers as part of 'families' are implicitly included throughout but a spotlight here may be useful. Serious case review analysis (Brandon, 2009) found that there was often a lack of information about men in assessments and records. More recently the failure to identify the roles of males in households was highlighted in the Baby Peter case indicating that workers can be more reluctant to engage with men and that there can be 'Rigid thinking about father figures as all good or all bad.' (Brandon, 2009). In child protection work, there can be a lack of consideration of the complexity of male roles in families, as social fathers or partners (Featherstone et al., 2014).

It is important to recognise that fathers may have different but significant parenting roles and that their involvement can vary with the age of the child. Also, men generally tend to be less involved with services, so more effort can be required with engagement. Ferguson (2011) suggests that the culture of agencies can move to being more 'father-inclusive' where the beliefs of workers seek to include what's important in children's lives, with men being both a source of risk and potential support. A useful resource on father's views and their engagement with children's services carried out on behalf of the Family Rights Group, *Fathers Matter action research projects*, can be found at http://www.frg.org.uk/fathers-matter-action-research-projects.

Social support

In considering social support itself, the theoretical underpinnings have developed, leading to a more defined, theorised and evidenced area of intervention that is based on the notion of support as the 'bread and butter of relationships' (Whittaker and Garbarino, 1983). The ideas are based on the premise that we all require support: early research in this area was carried out by Rutter (1985), who identified the protective nature of receiving support from others in helping people to cope and recover from adverse life events. Thinking around this area has developed significantly since this time and it is widely accepted as a core part of an individual's social ecology.

Social support is complex and is defined by Cutrona (1996: 17) as '...acts that demonstrate responsivity to another's need'. Cutrona (2000) had further suggested that there are four main types, which are practical, emotional, esteem and advice. Practical support can consist of material or financial assistance; emotional support often entails elements of empathy and listening, allowing a person to express and work through their emotions; esteem support looks to increasing a person's self-efficacy and image of themselves. The success of many interventions and services can be seen to be rooted in these basic but inherently useful ideas. Generally, it is a widely agreed goal of services to 'support' service users, which commonly involves elements associated with social capital (see below) such as building opportunities, self-efficacy and personal resources, usually leading to associated benefits in social functioning. An example of social support within an extended family network is from grandparents: this was highlighted in the *Growing up in Scotland* survey and has been fostered there with the development of the 'Charter for grandparents' (Gilligan, 2012).

What has been found to be key to social support is its quality, duration and type and the fact that it can be informal. Informal networks may be present but often need activating to obtain support (Gilligan, 2012). Formal social support refers to that provided by service, for example, a home care service providing social contact and practical help. Of course, it is the combination of different types that is required by service users and is most useful. The aim of services from a policy-and-outcomes-based perspective is often to increase the levels of people's informal assistance (through family and friends), which enables more long-term benefits and ensures that re-referrals to services are not required. This can make the steps forward from a service more sustainable: to establish links with both community and services that can increase families' sources of help in the longer term. This more developmental approach to social support is arguably an opportunity that could be more of an aim for services (Connolly, 2017).

An important part of these ideas is the actual perception of support and its durability. Social support and resilience are fundamental concepts in the field and are of significance in relation to the coping mechanisms of service users in various settings. Social support is important in terms of it being an ingredient of psychosocial well-being. In particular, its availability and also the person's perception of its availability assists the development of self-esteem and self-efficacy (Ghate and Hazel, 2002). Crucially, it also serves as a 'buffer' for stress when children experience adverse circumstances (McGrath et al., 2009).

A further useful concept here is reciprocity, which is a feature of the wider literature. Reciprocity is thought to enhance the effectiveness of social support itself and to provide unique benefits. In practice, if a service user receives help, the benefits can be increased if the person feels they are 'giving something back' or reciprocating, even in a very small way such as providing refreshment for a worker on a home visit. Reciprocity appears to make the assistance provided more effective (Cutrona, 2000), therefore it is an aspect that can usefully be considered by practitioners. It seems that reciprocity in itself can be seen as a useful goal, as it can act as a mediator of the effectiveness of social support (Nurullah, 2012).

Key point

Evidence suggests that service users generally value practical and emotional input (McKeown, 2013); furthermore, these can both be more effective when an element of reciprocity is introduced (Nurullah, 2012).

One of the main ideas in this area is that all of us need and utilise social support in our daily lives. As practitioners, understanding the value for ourselves, we can try to harness such valuable assets for service users.

Practice focus

It can often be complex when attempting to increase an individual's social networks; thus a variety of commonly employed tools exist for workers to measure and map out social support for individuals. The core methods are ecomaps, which are especially useful as they are completed in conjunction with the user, thereby encouraging empowerment. The maps can usefully be adapted for children, children with a disability and adolescents.

▶

◄

Such tools are not unproblematic, however, when dealing with more vulnerable families. It can often be the case that users may have very few informal networks. One example is that of care leavers who may have few contacts or extended family as young adults. Other families may live in poverty and be isolated from their community, and racism or language and cultural barriers may exist with the local area or community for some people. There may be a history of domestic violence or abuse within a family and perhaps intergenerational problems of mental health or substance misuse which can isolate family members from both their own extended family and the community. A number of factors influence how effective the provision of support is to more vulnerable families (Moran and Ghate, 2005).

A detailed outline of an ecomap, along with a template and example can also be found in *Assessing Children in Need and their Families: Practice Guidance* (Department of Health, 2000), page 30.

Consider how the ecomap might be produced with Evie and how it might look and be developed. She is originally from Poland and has been living on a small housing estate with her children aged 4 and 6 years: after separating from her partner Josh because of domestic abuse, some contact with him continues. Her sister lives a few hours away by train, and she still has contact with Josh's mother. With a thoughtful approach suggested given the considerations above, how might the ecomap help you to work with Evie? The ecomap could assist in developing further support networks – what might you consider here with Evie?

Messages from research

There is a good deal of writing on the role that mentoring can play, particularly youth mentoring (DuBois and Karcher, 2013). In working with adolescents, Dolan and Brady (2011) outline some of the benefits and the strong evidence base of improved outcomes from such intervention. There has been a rapid growth in mentoring practice, theory and research over recent years. Outcomes for young people are an increase in trust, reciprocity and participation and social support. There is also thought to be an increase overall of social capital.

Interestingly, Bracke et al. (2008), in examining peer support in a different setting, suggest that providing this is more beneficial than actually receiving it. This links to the earlier idea of reciprocity, suggesting that the benefits from such interventions where peer mentoring is an element may be multifaceted.

Resilience

This has emerged as a core concept in the family support field, and in services more widely. It was defined by Gilligan (2008) as the ability to 'bounce back' after psychosocial adversity, or to thrive despite facing adverse or difficult circumstances (Joslyn, 2015). It is central to the notion of family support primarily because it is one area that is most helpful to develop for those in contact with services. Secondly, it is useful because resilience can be built for individuals through practitioner intervention (Hughes et al., 2018), which makes it particularly crucial in practice terms. Early studies were carried out by Michael Rutter in the 1970s: researchers were essentially concerned to explore how and why some individuals managed to survive and sometimes thrive after traumatic experiences or difficult childhoods. It is pointed out that recovery from adversity in the key developmental stages of childhood but also at other points is possible. In this area, Gilligan (2000) looked at the experiences of children and young people in care and explored their coping strategies.

The ideas here are again universal ones, in that we all have coping strategies and the development of these is quite important to successful adaptation. Often our ability in this area is not shown until we are experiencing adversity, which could be due to multiple factors accumulating (Daniel et al., 2011). In other cases where crisis intervention might be useful after a catastrophic event, the development of resilience is important as part of recovery and as a turning point. Importantly, it is seen as being influenced by a number of factors rather than being mainly innate, or part of personality traits (Joslyn, 2015). Thinking around this area has developed to suggest that factors in a person's social ecology are crucial to developing this, such as culture (Ungar, 2008).

This concept is very applicable. On a practical level, schools can be an important source for young people: taking part in a hobby or sport with achievement helps to build self-esteem (Daniel et al., 2011). Unconditional support from a key adult outside the family can boost resilience (Sawyer and Burton, 2016) and children can be facilitated to develop more positive rather than maladaptive and short-term coping mechanisms (Pearce, 2011). Similarly, for adults, after a difficult upbringing, such maladaptive coping strategies can include substance/alcohol misuse, and by understanding how these patterns develop, services can better respond.

Key point

The perceived ability to cope is important, by providing a sense of hope and the belief that a person can deal with an issue. Increasingly, attention is being drawn to resilience and on the internal and external factors that could contribute to it. Crucial here is the thinking that it can be built through intervention (Brooks, 2006; Dolan, 2006).

An important aspect here is the balance between resilience in the face of difficult experiences and continued risk and vulnerability. Critiques have emerged, for example in relation to a neglected child who may find coping mechanisms but remain in the same family situation and may not in fact be doing well in the long run (Hill et al., 2007). Whilst it can be seen that building resilience for people is empowering and linked to social justice, others argue it can encourage people to accept the 'status quo'. One example would be to encourage a person to adapt to circumstances of poverty or low income and become resilient rather than take an approach of alleviating their situation: advocates of family support can take a socially just position on this.

Resilience as the product of experiencing difficulty will continue to be controversial, as developing it effectively may require some exposure to the stressor (Ungar, 2008). Joslyn (2015) summarises key research in this area: whilst we accept that sustained or cumulative adversity is unhealthy, the level of resilience developed will vary between individuals, with factors such as the support networks around them having an influence.

Practice focus

Practitioners in children's services commonly draw on this for children in or leaving the care system – the research around children in care and leaving care has been extensive. In terms of developing resilience and social support for often vulnerable young people, the size and importantly the quality of the network can be directly related to how much resilience a young person is able to develop. It can also be built by a child/young person having an additional role or interest outside the home environment, where they can achieve and bolster their self-confidence.

Consider Jasmine aged 10 years who is part of the family outlined in the practice focus in Chapter 2. The household is likely to be quite busy on a daily basis and the family are dealing with a number of issues. As a quieter child, in the middle of the age range, Jasmine's needs might get 'lost'. What could you consider outside the home that could provide Jasmine with another role outside the family? Perhaps at school or in a local group, an activity based on Jasmine's interests could enable her to have a role as member of a dance/music group; or in school being given a small responsibility in the classroom, either of which could boost her self-esteem and build resilience.

International examples

Mels et al. (2008) examined the social support networks of unaccompanied asylum-seeking boys in Belgium. There was a concern for the overall well-being of the group who had often endured trauma in their country of origin, difficult journeys and separation from home, family and community. They found that increasing the amount of social support appeared to indirectly enhance their well-being through providing them with increased coping abilities. Furthermore, the additional input appeared to operate at a direct level through increased social contact and self-esteem, thereby improving the psychosocial functioning of the boys.

This study suggests that a focus on social networks is important and could be part of an intervention for this group. At an international level, it also highlights the transnational aspect of the boys' lives, an aspect that has become increasingly important in the context of asylum-seeking and refugee children and increased migration in general (Christie and Walsh, 2015). These issues suggest the transferability of the ideas across complex settings in many countries.

Ecological systems theory

Ecological systems is generally seen as the overarching theory that underpins work in the family support area. Both general systems and ecological theory were brought together most famously by Urie Bronfenbrenner in his ecological systems theory (2009). The ideas of systems have been widely used, essentially looking at how components intersect and affect and influence each other. In the early stages of the emergence of this area (the 1970s) it was seen as a departure from the more traditional methods which viewed family problems and their solutions as rooted in individual pathology, an approach that had dominated service provision for a number of decades (Walker, 2015).

Systems thinking was utilised in terms of seeing the family as a system where the component parts both interact and affect one another, but Bronfenbrenner also saw the individual and the family as part of a wider system (Rixon, 2011). It is seen as particularly useful as it draws on concepts which are easily recognisable and is generally depicted as a diagram of concentric circles indicating the micro, meso and macro layers of a person's social environment at its simplest form; he later added the more complex exo and chrono levels to enhance the model.

Micro-system: Child at
the centre, significant
relationships e.g. family

Meso-system: Home,
School, Neighbourhood

Exo-system: e.g. parents'
workplace

Macrosystem:
Wider society,
government policy

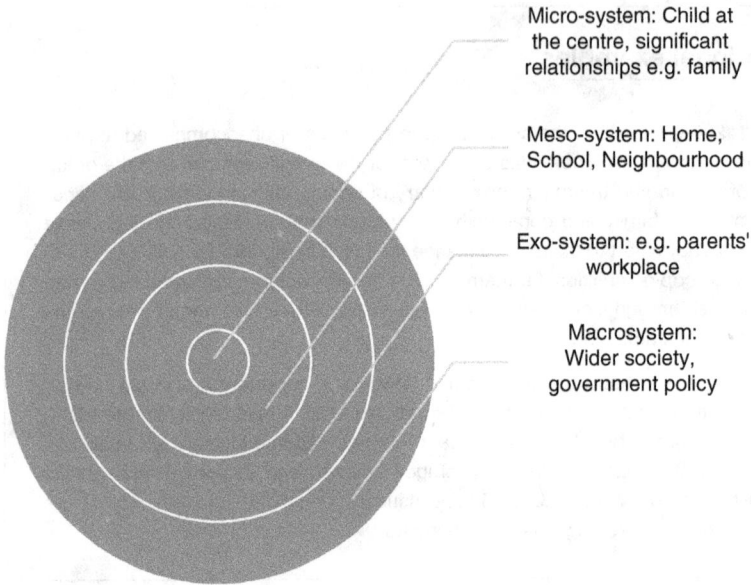

A number of practice applications such as ecomaps are based on these ideas as discussed earlier. As tools they are also very accessible to the service user and can serve to promote empowerment. One of the particularly useful aspects of this is the ability to incorporate a range of social and psychological factors into the mapping. This is quite readily achieved because of the inclusion of both the micro or personal layers along with the much wider layers at the wider community level. Considering a brief example: attachment operates at the micro level for individuals but can be influenced by macro and meso factors, such as the effects of poverty and stress on parenting, which can affect the quality of relationships and attachments between parents and their children (Daniel et al., 2011). In terms of services, the Family Nurse Partnership aimed at disadvantaged first-time mothers is an example of a well-evaluated ecologically based application (Jack and Donnellan, 2013). O'Sullivan (2012) outlines an ecological model applied to parenting, in which social networks are important to consider both for support and also stress factors such as work. This enables better input with families as strengths and areas for support can be considered.

This set of ideas or conceptualisation of the individual within their wider environment has become central to all assessments carried out in the children and families arena in particular. The theory underpins the *Framework of Assessment for Children in Need and their Families* and now the *Working Together to Safeguard Children* (2018) and associated documents as well as the assessment frameworks in the other UK countries and Ireland. It provided a means to view the child as a central part of a wider family, a community, and to consider the range of factors that influence families such as housing and poverty (Jack and Gill, 2010).

The ecological systems approach is generally a more optimistic lens – seeking to identify areas where strengths could be enhanced, as opposed to the former, more individualistic view (Jack, 1997). It can also be developmental and empowering for the service user: this is because the focus is not just on individual factors in its outlook, but it seeks to include wider issues and explanations. It can be argued that it did herald a change to a more person-centred approach. In some ways it has become almost implicit in a range of health and social care areas. The terminology of Bronfenbrenner is widely used in discussing the macro issues in spheres of community development and the addition of the chrono-system was particularly useful in giving a life course and inter-generational perspective.

Key point

There are strong links from the outset with social justice, particularly in the acknowledgment of poverty and the environment. However, there are critiques that often the ecological system's perspective does not give wider factors sufficient weight (Rixon, 2011; O'Sullivan, 2012). Given the pressures on individuals and families living with poverty, inequality and austerity measures, this is a timely and crucial focus (Dolan et al., 2015).

Practice focus

Linking to the earlier idea of resilience, we know from ecological systems theory that stressors from different sources can occur. Stressors can have a purely environmental cause such as housing, unemployment or poverty. Or a stressor could be quite personal in nature and operate at the micro level, for example, a family break-up. The principles of social justice suggest that many people who come to the attention of services have typically had a number of difficult and sometimes catastrophic experiences, so helping them cope and overcome or be able to cope with these is crucial.

Considering the family discussed in Chapter 2, we know that Georgina had been physically abused and neglected as a child and has recently been depressed. The family support worker has found through engaging with Georgina that she had run

▶

◄

away from home frequently as a teenager and often slept in a nearby shed. Having little wider family input, the violence in her first relationship led to low self-esteem, which has continued for Georgina. Added to this over the years have been numerous financial stresses and health issues in the family, which has left her with a decreased ability to cope; she feels that 'things always go wrong in this family'. Considering this social justice perspective, what areas could the worker look at to build Georgina's resilience that would impact on the family as a whole?

Key point

Returning to the earlier discussion and the use of ecomaps: these can show the number but also the strength and durability of people's relationships. The important concept here is that this is from the perspective of the user themselves: showing who is important to the person, what kind of relationships exist and what factors affect this. Here we can explore the most valued aspects of relationships with others like being listened to, having empathy shown and having a sense of genuine caring, which can come from different sources.

Social capital

The ideas of social capital became popular in the US from the 1980s onwards after they were set out by Coleman (1988) and Putnam (1993), who both primarily focussed on social networks and how these benefit people and organisations. Bourdieu had identified social capital as a potential resource both at the individual and the community level, which he described as building supportive alliances and creating access to social resources (Bourdieu, 2011). It can be defined as the individual and social benefits that come from developing social networks, particularly those based around trust (Rohe, 2004), and may be described as a kind of beneficial by-product of social interactions and connections.

The theoretical ideas of social and human capital have become integral to both the rationale and practice of many services to children and their families. There is a potential benefit in terms of conceptualising how we can expand people's networks: increasing the social capital of individuals from various groups in society is an aim of much social policy (see, e.g., Healy and Cotes, OECD, 2001). A distinction between 'bonding' and 'bridging' social capital has been made, with bonding related to social ties and networks between individuals and even within an extended family: this type tends to strengthen relationships. Bridging emphasises 'vertical' links to other networks and resources that can be accessed outside the immediate family/community and provides links to outside opportunities and resources; in other words bonding is about 'getting by' and bridging about 'getting ahead' (Frost and Dolan, 2012). Civic or community engagement by individuals that provides them with increased ties to their community or to society as a whole is an example of this in action. Hawkins and Maurer (2011) suggest that in practice, social workers can usefully apply this by linking networks and support for people: an important pointer for services. In relation to children and young people, a thought-provoking overview of the relevance here is provided by Holland (2008), which includes different communities and a specific reference to a Northern Ireland study.

Critiques have noted its often gender blind and limited application by some theorists that may not consider social justice, such as intersectional disadvantage that may limit women's access to networks outside the home sphere. Belcher et al. (2011), for example, point out that in terms of the related notion of family capital, it can be harder for those in poverty to gain this due to more limited access to wider services and contacts, restricted by household budget.

Poverty puts a strain on social networks and reduces opportunities for them to develop, resulting in big differences with affluent communities (Matthews and Besemer, 2015). Building social capital for poor and marginalised communities is complex and there can be a number of social factors that influence how much networks actually translate into capital that is useful for individuals and families (Boon and Farnsworth, 2011).

Practice focus

Ann is a lone parent who had been in a relationship where there was domestic abuse for a number of years. Her family support worker helped her to start some voluntary work with isolated migrant women for a charity, a few hours per week. She gained another role, which in psychological terms was beneficial as it increased her self-esteem; it also added a protective factor in terms of developing resilience, through having multiple social roles. After being in receipt of help from services herself, feeling the sense of reciprocity in being able to 'give something back' was very beneficial for Ann.

She gained new social networks from this experience and through a contact there was later able to move onto paid part-time employment. This improved her financial status and also meant she was taking an more active part in civil society: this shows a multiplicity of benefits at both the individual and the community levels.

Human development and attachment theories

Relationships are a vital part of human growth and development across the lifespan, providing the basis of support and underpinning our social/ emotional functioning (Howe, 2011). Attachment theory is useful to consider in thinking about relationship forming; it involves the study of human relationships and particularly early, formative ones. Bowlby's original writings in the 1950s looked beyond the physical care of infants, to innate bonds that developed between a child and their caregiver, suggesting that there was a biological imperative in the infant to form attachments and exhibit behaviour to promote this (see Bowlby, 2005). Theories of attachment have been an important part of work with children and families and have informed assessment and intervention. There is a wealth of literature around attachment particularly where children are or have been in care, although Aldgate (2015) suggests a positive strength-based application of attachment theory as it has often been used to justify a range of policy and practice particularly around children in the care system.

A clear knowledge of attachment styles is crucial both to inform parenting and to understand the adults' response to their children. Children who show signs of disorganised attachment, for example, may have parents or carers who exhibit some characteristics such as unresolved trauma or loss, very disconnected or insensitive parenting and low abilities of mentalization (Shemmings and Shemmings, 2014). A number of different assessments can be carried out by practitioners around attachment, with the aim of being able to provide a more specific and preventative approach to working with individuals and families; a useful link can be found at http://arpractice.org.uk/index.html.

Different patterns of adult attachment, based on childhood experiences, are well documented. It has been shown that these patterns have an influence on our relationship forming throughout later life (see Howe, 2011). Clearly, this factor could affect a service user's ability to form a working relationship with a practitioner or key worker. Other factors can also be at play that can influence relationship forming: Sheppard (2002) found that engagement with workers was affected by depression for some mothers involved in services. Fear of disappointment and lack of trust can be an issue for vulnerable service users in forming close personal relationships generally, which can result in a more restricted pool of social support; also, the durability and reliability can take longer to establish. A useful example of a project that has incorporated attachment and therapeutic ideas is Love Barrow Families, set up in a northern England area. This service is for individual families but set within a community approach and it aims to utilise both adult and child attachment assessments alongside staple family and community supports to capture the complex and intersecting needs of disadvantaged families (Robson et al., 2015).

Key point

The ability to accept and benefit from social support can be affected by attachment patterns. The helping and supporting relationship can trigger attachment behaviours and individuals can respond negatively, or perhaps be unable to sustain a consistent and ongoing relationship. Given that a large proportion of service users will themselves be from neglected backgrounds or have mental health/substance misuse issues, this is an area where practitioners in the field can play an important role.

Key tension for reflection: The child-centred/family tension in family support

A child-centred approach has become the main concern of protection services, whilst the focus of family support is widely seen as the family and the child within this. However, some argue that this child-centred lens can become an unhelpful way to view child welfare when the child is viewed in isolation: Featherstone et al. (2014: 139) describe this as the '...uncoupling of the child from kin...'.

The theoretical perspectives of family support suggest that children's rights are crucial, but that the wider ecological perspective also requires an emphasis on relationships and networks for the child both in the present and future contexts. As Bronfenbrenner (1974: 57) noted in reviewing successful early years services: '...approaches that are family-centred rather than child-centred, that cut across contexts rather than being confined to a single setting...'. Various writers have stressed the positive effects in reducing child maltreatment and promoting children's welfare through effective family support with parents (Gardner, 2002; Whittaker and Garbarino, 1983) and more recently, in the US, Martin, Gardner and Brooks Gunn (2012).

It is crucial for family support to maintain this lens on the child's voice and welfare whilst emphasising the familial and relational context of the child's world.

Further reading

Featherstone, B., 2003. *Family Life and Family Support: A Feminist Analysis* (Introduction: pp. 1–13). Palgrave Macmillan.
This introductory chapter sets out some of the key terms and issues with a critical approach.

Health Equity Evidence Review 2: September 2014. *Local Action on Health Inequalities: Building Children and Young People's Resilience in Schools*. Public Health England.
As an evidence review, this gives a perspective on resilience during childhood that can be built on and developed.

Howe, D., 2011. *Attachment Across the Lifecourse: A Brief Introduction*. Palgrave Macmillan.
A key text that covers the theory and practical application of attachment.

Joslyn, E., 2015. *Resilience in Childhood: Perspectives, Promise & Practice*. Palgrave Macmillan.
A thorough outline of resilience theory and research is covered in this recent book.

Martin, G., Gardner, M. & Brooks, G.J., 2012. The mediated and moderated effects of family support on child maltreatment. *Journal of Family Studies, 33*(7), 920–941.
This article provides an interesting perspective examining the possibilities from links between support and child protection.

Race, T. & O'Keefe, R., 2017. *Child-Centred Practice: A Handbook for Social Work*. Palgrave.
This recent publication provides a thorough coverage for practice application from a clear child-centered perspective.

PART 2

Practice and Service Users

4

Family Support Practice with Children and Families

Although family support in the children's arena often has a lower profile than child protection work, it is a crucial area of work with children and it is often the largest part of practice undertaken in the sector. In taking a holistic and multidisciplinary perspective, some of the tensions in balancing support for families and children with protection will be explored as key themes. The issues of early intervention and prevention form the policy backdrop to this area and these ideas have framed recent debates and discussions. This chapter will also provide an overview of some specific areas from a family support perspective.

The chapter will cover:

➤ Child protection and welfare

➤ Supporting families

➤ Holistic family perspectives and family group conferences

➤ The role of a 'team around the family/child'; the common assessment framework; early help

➤ Children with a disability or additional needs

➤ Children with mental health problems

➤ Young carers

➤ Young people leaving care and aftercare support

➤ 'Troubled' families

➤ *Key tension for reflection: Family support and safeguarding – a focused approach rather than a softer option*

Child protection and welfare

In terms of the legislative and policy framework in relation to child protection, the principles of the primary legislation underpin the whole approach to children and their families as well as providing the outline of responsibilities in the area (the Children Act 1989 in England and Wales). The document that outlines the responses that should be taken following a referral of a concern about a child in England are set out in the statutory guidance: 'Working together to safeguard children' (2018) (WTSC); similarly, statutory guidance on safeguarding children, which includes child protection procedures, is outlined in Wales in the Safeguarding Children: Working Together under the Children Act 2004, in Scotland as the 'National Guidance for Child Protection in Scotland' (2014), in Northern Ireland as 'Co-operating to Safeguard Children and Young People in Northern Ireland' (2017) and in Ireland as 'Children First: National Guidance for the Protection and Welfare of Children' (2011). It is guidance that applies to the wider safeguarding functions, but also more specifically it sets out child protection processes.

In relation to considering child protection, section 47 of the Children Act 1989 is the key component in England and Wales as it deals with children who are suffering or likely to suffer significant harm. Central to the legislation in terms of protection is this concept of harm, which is defined but not prescribed – in considering risk and the threshold, it is a matter of professional judgement based on a sound assessment that takes a child-centred and multidisciplinary approach. It was suggested in WTSC 2013 that there is no exact way to assess significant harm and the following points were suggested to help assess this:

➢ The age and development of the child – do they have a disability or any special needs?

➢ The capacity of the parents to care for the child

➢ The nature of the harm – how serious is it?

➢ The duration of the harm – is it a one-off incident?

➢ Any protective factors or strengths?

➢ Are the family previously known?

➢ Are there any other risk factors present?

➢ The response of the parents/carer

➢ The child's own views and the effect on them (adapted from WTSC, 2013)

The notion of safeguarding was an attempt to widen the scope of child protection and broaden responsibility to the multiprofessional arena. The protection of children from abuse, maltreatment and neglect is one of the core areas of work in the safeguarding field. For the four categories of child abuse, namely physical, sexual, emotional and neglect, local authorities follow the specific processes and procedures in dealing with referrals of maltreatment which are rooted in the primary laws and associated statutory guidance mentioned above. Protecting children where there are concerns that there may be significant harm, or a risk of this, is an essential component of safeguarding activity overall.

The 'child in need' is defined in section 17 of the Children Act 1989 and services must be provided for such children where families consent, although the extent of the provision is not specified. Much of the work with children and families takes place at this child in need level, also at the wider child welfare level (through the CAF, see below) or at the preventative end of the spectrum, below the threshold of significant harm. Systems in Scotland (GIRFEC) and Ireland (TUSLA) follow a similar pattern in attempting to provide assessment and services on a broader welfare and often preventative basis. Work with children and their families at these levels is undertaken by a range of professionals and para-professionals. Child welfare can then be seen as the broader term – covering the physical, social, emotional and developmental needs of children and young people.

Key point

The concept of significant harm, as outlined above, is relevant here as it is mediated by various factors. Some regions are trying to develop more holistic and all-encompassing orientations to child welfare, such as restorative practice and other 'strengthening families' models. These attempt to address whole family needs, taking some of these factors into account. The aim is to take a more preventative stance, where families receive help earlier, with the idea of preventing later more protective action. This is an example of the use of *prevention* to try and effectively target services across the spectrum of need by taking a broader view.

Messages from research

The *Messages from Research* series has consistently published important findings in relation to our understanding of child welfare, child abuse and neglect. The volume from Davies and Ward (2011) contains a range of studies and a link is available on

▶

◀

the Department for Education website: https://www.gov.uk/government/publications/safeguarding-children-across-services-messages-from-research.

The original *Messages from Research* were a turning point in 1995, showing us that a focus on the investigative aspects of the child protection system had developed following the Children Act. This landmark publication led to a debate about the reconfiguring of service approaches, which arguably continues today and is often described as the pendulum swinging between investigative child protection and a more supportive stance.

Similarly, the pieces of research in the series that focus on emotional abuse and neglect, both its features and its consequences for younger children and older adolescents, are a thought-provoking and topical read. Here, the issues from different perspectives are considered.

Supporting families

The core functions of protecting and safeguarding children and the wider functions of promoting children's welfare and providing support are commonly viewed as a continuum of intervention. Most local authorities in the UK and elsewhere have what can be described as different levels of services across this, from universal need to the protective or remedial end. This is seen as a useful way of targeting services to meet need, for example, remedial and protective services for children who are in need of protection or who have been maltreated and may be in alternative care. Services for children in need or with more complex needs comprise the next level, with lower level input for simpler needs and then services that are primarily preventative and are available to all. Hardiker, Exton and Barker's well-known model (1991) depicts the different levels of intervention and the decreasing numbers of children and families that are involved towards the more protective end. The distinction between universal, tertiary and remedial services is an example of this model in action and is seen as being a widely used and useful application.

Key point

The idea of a continuum or levels of services continues to be a very useful conceptual model. However, the model may have become more limited in terms of being used primarily to apply thresholds to services (Frost et al., 2015).

▶

Level 1	Level 2	Level 3	Level 4
Everyday needs all children/ Universal	Simple support needs (Common Assessment Framework/ Early Help), targeted to early difficulties/risk	Complex support needs (S.17) children with difficulties/at risk	Child protection (S.47), children at risk/specialist intervention

Decreasing numbers of children ⟶

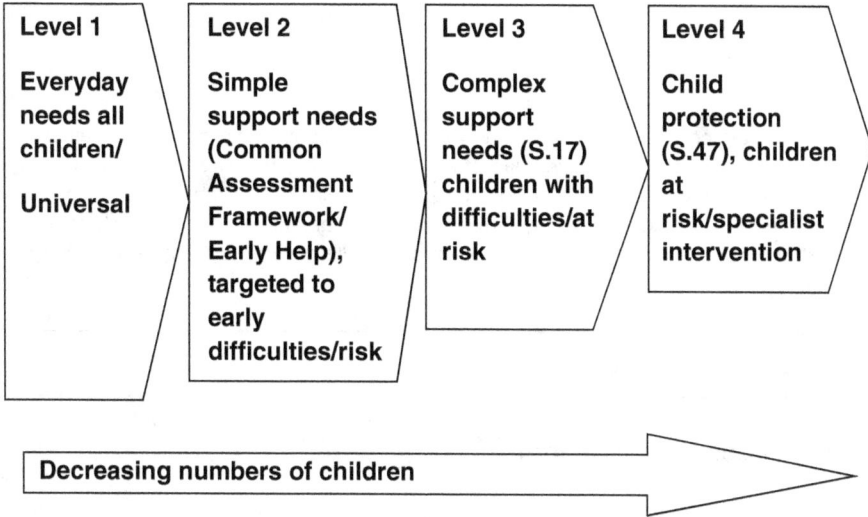

Source: Adapted from Hardiker et al. (1991)

◀

There are also a number of complexities – for example, with the concept of prevention, which has been referred to earlier. Prevention has been discussed in the context
of universally available services and also in the context of preventing difficulties for
families becoming worse, as a narrower application of the idea. The complexity of
these applications and some suggested analysis from the field will be discussed
further.

There have been many policy-level attempts and practice initiatives
aimed at efforts to strengthen families and work holistically to prevent
families becoming the subject of higher level intervention, such as the
'Think Family' approach or variations of 'strengthening families'. This
certainly fits in with a family rights perspective, so that help is provided
where it is needed, before issues escalate to the more remedial end.
An important current issue that will be considered in the concluding
chapter is the matter of policy in the context of funding priorities, which
has seen more of a focus at the higher need/risk end where statutory
duties lie, whereas more supportive services have been prone to cutbacks
in funding in recent times.

Key point

Although the continuum idea is useful, viewing family support as an *ideology*, rather than as a point in time or a fixed part of the spectrum, may be more helpful, fitting in with the points highlighted in previous chapters. Its applicability is best seen across the spectrum, for example, using some of the theory and principles of a family support approach at the child protection level to promote engagement and relationship building.

Messages from research

Key factors from serious case reviews (SCRs)

Analyses of SCRs reveal some patterns in terms of key factors in families that were present in these cases. The *Audit and Analysis of Significant Case Reviews* carried out on behalf of the Scottish Government (Vincent and Petch, 2012) showed that some family factors were:

- Over one-third of parents considered to have had troubled childhoods

- Two-thirds of cases featured parental substance misuse

- One-half of cases featured domestic abuse

- Over 40% of cases featured parental mental health issues

- Over one-half of families held criminal records for serious offences involving violence or drugs

These issues that have similarly shown as features in other analyses (see Sidebotham et al., 2016) are not in themselves either an indicator or predictor of child abuse. They do, however, illustrate the complex wider welfare issues that are involved in considering child protection. A more recent analysis of SCRs in Scotland has again highlighted the issues of parental substance misuse and criminality as features of the cases (Vincent and Petch, 2017).

Holistic family perspectives and family group conferences

In policy terms, holistic family ideas have gained much prominence in recent decades. These have become widely implemented in different forms, for example, whole family perspectives (Malin et al., 2014).

A crucial aspect of 'Think Family' that developed in mental health services is that all agencies and services, including adult-based services, recognise that issues have an impact on the whole family. The general principles of the delivery of family support are that:

➢ it is available for all families who need it;

➢ no stigma is attached to the help provided;

➢ support is across the board (wide-ranging and joined-up between agencies); and

➢ it is accessible to families and young people.

(adapted from Shaw and Frost, 2013)

The development of a range of more holistic approaches across services is to be welcomed, particularly for their family-centred rather than service-centred emphasis. However, there has been a general trend for these to become more targeted and associated with higher risk families (Morris, 2011).

An important whole family model that has grown in its use is the family group conference (FGC). Originating in New Zealand, the family group conference has been widely implemented across a number of countries. The model is rooted in a holistic family-focused, strengths-based and empowering perspective. It aims to involve wider family members and mobilize resources within the family. The family group conference (or family welfare conference as it is known in some areas, such as Ireland) is a meeting convened to devise a family plan: it is usually coordinated by a facilitator who brings together family members and significant others, along with professionals. The main issue or concern is usually distilled into a 'bottom line' around risk that must be addressed. The main difference with a traditional meeting is that the family has devoted private or family time where they discuss and come up with an action plan without the input of professionals.

FGCs were introduced a number of years ago and there has been literature around their implementation and effectiveness over the last few decades (see Morris and Tunnard, 1996; Marsh and Crow, 1998). Evaluations have shown that the conferences are a preferred model for both families and children and young people in terms of being listened to (Holland et al., 2005). There has been a recent growth in interest in FCGs as a form of more participatory and engaging practice (Morris, 2011): the growing use of FGCs in child protection cases in the UK has led to their more widespread use, although it may move the focus from engagement to outcomes in such cases. The Family Rights Group in the UK is an organization that promotes and provides information, advice and training around FGCs – their website is available at: http://www.frg.org.uk. In Chapter 8, an example of recent innovative services that are utilizing an FGC model is explored.

Role of the team around the family and child, the common assessment framework (CAF) and early help

Local authorities organize their services in different ways, but generally screen referrals in line with the flow charts detailed in the WTSC 2018, which show the pathway of a referral at the various stages, with similar variants in Wales, Scotland and Northern Ireland. Some referrals may not be accepted as having sufficient concerns of significant harm and may be recorded as 'no further action' or referred to another agency such as CAMHs or family support services. Others may be discussed in terms of signposting to other services or the referrer may be advised that a CAF/Early Help assessment should be carried out if there are some complex needs (see the diagram above). In the case of higher level concerns being identified through this, the CAF may be accepted as referral in itself although the guidance is clear that it is not a prerequisite to making a referral.

The CAF came into operation after the Children Act 2004 and the first Laming report (2003) and was an attempt to widen the responsibility for child welfare assessments to a range of key professionals and also to ensure that needs were identified at an earlier stage. The CAF also drew on the existing assessment framework and the WTSC statutory guidance, utilising an ecological systems approach. In many areas, the term CAF is being replaced by an 'Early Help' assessment. Evaluations of the use and effectiveness of the CAF have been carried out, with a study in the LARC series finding that children and families received help for their difficulties earlier and that a range of better outcomes were reported (Easton et al., 2011).

The team around the child or family (TAC/TAF) has also become an important part of this attempt to share responsibility for child welfare and to maximise services for children. The inter-agency working is vital to this process, with meetings regularly reviewed to provide clear assessment, intervention, multi-agency input and a partnership with families. The principles of the TAF/TAC model are that the child is central to the process in terms of their needs and protection, meetings should be clear and involve the family and all practitioners involved in support attend and share responsibility. The process relies on the skill, experience and commitment of different workers who are involved with a family. Important ingredients include providing a less formal atmosphere for meetings, having clear roles, goals, and timescales and good attendance by families and practitioners, and being clear about needs (Institute of Public Care, 2011).

The ideas behind early help itself were set out on the Children Act 1989/2004 which emphasised early intervention, prevention and inter-agency collaboration. Early help is the broader term which considers support early on when a problem or issues emerges. As explained in WTSC 2015, it can be provided as problems emerge, which can be at any point in a child's life. Its importance as an approach was set out in the Munro review of child protection, which emphasised that preventative services were important in dealing with child abuse and neglect rather than reactive services (Munro, 2011).

Key point

The Munro review (2011) is one of the main reports that has emphasised the role of prevention and early help. More recently, Action for Children have summarised that:

There has been an enduring debate over the past two decades about whether services should take a preventive approach or focus on crisis intervention. We are starting to see a broad consensus…that intervening early with effective support when problems first arise. (Action for Children, 2013).

However, their report also points out that this is in the context of retrenched resources for services in many jurisdictions.

Practice focus

The Early Help approach in Leeds is an example of a proactive service for children and their families. The term replaces the previous CAF process and describes what practitioners should do in practice preceding a social care referral. The principles of the Early Help approach are:

'Conversations' should take place within and between universal, targeted and specialist Services

- A lead Professional should oversee an Early Help assessment
- Targeted Services are available through clusters in each area
- Services for adults should be considered, using a' Think Family' approach
- An Early Help assessment can become a referral to social care

(*Source*: Adapted from Leeds City Council)

Messages from research

Research in recent years has emphasised the benefits of an increased focus on early intervention services. More specifically, a recognition of the role of preventative input has been highlighted: the Munro Review (2011) highlighted early help for families and although criticized for some aspects, the Allen Review (2011) pulled together some arguments in this regard.

Additionally, service evaluations from the family support arena have highlighted different provisions and which elements of these work well (see Vincent, 2015). There has been a general growth of evidence-based practice in services and a concern about value for money and evidencing outcomes. Although this book proposes that the value of family support is wider than individual programme evaluation, the growing base of informed research and evidence provides useful information about the elements of practitioners' work with families.

An overview report on early intervention from a practice perspective is available from C4EO, which contains a series of 'key messages':

Grasping the nettle: early intervention for children, families and communities. Available at: http://www.c4eo.org.uk/themes/earlyintervention/files/early_intervention_grasping_the_nettle_full_report.pdf.

Key point: Where does *early help* fit in?

Early help can be delivered to children and their families through existing universal services and/or targeted services. It aims to deal with problems and issues as they are emerging, at the earliest stage possible. This means that early help is not just targeted at the early years' child, but can be at any stage of childhood or adolescence. An additional benefit of early help is that families who are identified as being potentially at risk of developing problems can be engaged. Early help is a wider term that focuses on support, rather than 'early intervention', which has a narrower focus (Frost et al., 2015).

Practice focus

This case scenario is set in a school, where pastoral staff can be crucial in working with young people. Tom is a young person aged 14 years (DOB 15/03/03); he has previously been referred to CAMHs but has been reluctant to engage. He is now refusing to attend school and is reluctant to leave the house due to social anxiety. It has also come to light that he has threatened his mum and sister Holly (aged 7).

▶

◀

In this case, after the school safeguarding officer reported the concerns to the local authority, the school was asked to undertake a CAF or Early Help assessment. What factors would you be exploring during this assessment to find out about Tom's profile and story and how the children are parented and cared for?

Below are suggested questions and approaches:

- What is happening for the child and family? How are they managing? Why the referral?

- Family functioning

- Other agencies or services involved

- Family and child strengths and protective factors: What is working well? What are we worried about?

- Risks for the child – What could happen if nothing changes?

- Analysis: What do we think should happen?

- Looking to the future: how will we know things have worked?

- Outcomes we want for the child(ren)

Parents and children's views

Children with a disability or additional needs

A disabled child can be offered assessment and services as a child in need under section 17 of the Children Act 1989; however the services offered may be variable. As Kirton (2008) has argued, the inclusion in the Act of the statutory duty to provide support says little about the amount and quality of this. One example here is short breaks which are provided to families as short periods of help in the home or as respite breaks. This is an important area in terms of children and young people's provision where services are provided, and the multiplicity of benefits for children, their parents and siblings are well documented (Collins et al., 2013). A recent study commissioned in Scotland by the commissioner for children and young people found that families were experiencing cutbacks in services across the board and a move to more crisis-oriented approaches rather than preventative input (Stalker et al., 2015).

Approximately 7.3% of UK children are thought to be disabled according to official definitions but this figure does not reflect the varied and heterogeneous nature of disability (The Council for Disabled Children). These figures are not consistently represented nationally in 'Child in Need' statistics, with just 9.4% at assessment characterised as primarily due to 'Child's disability or illness' at assessment in 2017 (Department for Education). There are also quite large variations in these numbers between local authorities, suggesting differences locally in eligibility, thresholds and organisation of services regionally (Council for Disabled Children). The Council for Disabled Children and the True Colours Trust have used existing data to estimate that the number of disabled children in schools with complex needs and/or life-limiting conditions has doubled since 2004 to over 70,000 (Pinney, 2016). Higher poverty levels, greater financial hardship and often housing and transport difficulties exist for families of children with disabilities (Blackburn et al., 2010; Jack and Donnellan, 2013).

The statutory guidance outlines that there are a proportionally higher number of children with a disability who are subject to abuse and neglect, which is an important issue for practitioners to be aware of. Disabled children have particular vulnerabilities due to a number of factors such as communication issues, being dependent on others for daily physical care, sometimes being cared for away from home, and stress in the family environment (Daniel et al., 2011). A level of knowledge and awareness for disabled children's needs is important for practitioners, along with an ability to communicate with a range of children using different tools (Winter, 2010).

The majority of input with disabled children and their families is in the area of support. The evidence base of research in this area emphasises the principles of empowerment for both the child or young person and their family and of seeing the child first. This had been reflected in the 'Aiming High for Disabled Children: Better Support for Families' policy (2007) and 'Caring Together: The Carers Strategy for Scotland' (2010–2015). Provision for families that is experienced as being empowering helps to build parents' capacity to cope and increases their self-efficacy. A range of formal and informal input is seen as crucial here, with a whole family perspective taken; siblings also face additional pressures, therefore a systemic and whole-family thinking is important (Seligman and Darling, 2017). For children and young people themselves, a whole-child focus is crucial, with wider social factors, for example inclusion and their own sense of self, being considered. It is suggested that communication with children should include an emphasis on their rights and challenging discrimination and exclusion (Winter, 2010). A recent study of young people's views in Scotland found that a number experienced a sense of exclusion particularly around friendships and peer activities (Sylvester et al., 2014), whilst another review similarly noted a sense of exclusion from out of school activities (Knight et al., 2014).

In terms of legislation and policy in the UK, the Children and Families Act 2014 has amended the Children Act 1989 and now requires local councils to assess carers of children where an assessment was requested by the parent or on the appearance of need. Assessments for disabled children continue to be carried out under the Children Act 1989 across the UK, with local authorities having a duty to assess children in need under the age of 18 for any services that they or their families may need. However, along with the above point, charges can apply for these services. The Care Act 2014 covers provision for carers and for the children and young people who are approaching age 18 years where they would 'transition' into adult-based services. Again, local authorities are required to provide assistance and planning. For children with special educational needs, the new Children and Families Act 2014 has put in place education, health and care (EHC) plans. The Special Educational Needs and Disabilities (SEND) system follows new statutory requirements under the Act that local services work together to provide care and input for children and young people with needs and disabilities. In Scotland there is a similar requirement for a child to have a plan: there, the Children and Young People Act 2014 included the requirement for a named person to co-ordinate services for a child. The 'Special Educational Needs Code of Practice for Wales' provides an overview of guidance for Welsh services in this area.

International example

Tétreault et al. (2014) have provided an international overview, across a number of countries, of helpful provision to families in which there is a disabled child. They document some of the issues that families face, such as financial difficulties, stresses of caring and higher levels of poverty. The types of service provided to families across different countries are categorized, and the authors suggest they broadly fall into the areas of respite services, child minding, emergency provision and support. In the category of support there are a number of areas suggested, which include practical help, financial assistance, legal and information provision and educational assistance.

This analysis is potentially beneficial for families and for practitioners within services in terms of characterizing what input might be needed by families across the spectrum of need.

Young carers

This term refers to children under the age of 18 years with caring responsibilities. There are estimated to be around 700,000 young carers in the UK at present (The Carers Trust). Children's needs and welfare are covered in the UK by the provisions of assessment in the Children Act 1989 and the more recent Children and Families Act 2014. The latest act has given more responsibility to local authorities to identify such children. This group of young people has become widely recognised in terms of their needs, with research showing the wishes of children and young people to be recognised and supported. A landmark report by Dearden and Becker, *Young Carers in the UK: the 2004 Report,* provided a comprehensive outline of the characteristics of young carers and the nature of their caring roles. In terms of children's views about what works well, a participatory study carried out by McAndrew et al. (2012) identified social support and coping strategies for young carers. A whole-family lens that looks at the impacts on family members, wider family and the social context of caring is the most helpful approach where a parent has mental health difficulties (Glasby and Tew, 2015); young carers for parents with a mental health problem may be affected in terms of their own mental well-being where stress and stigma are factors.

International example

The study by Fives, Kennan, Canavan, Brady and Kearns titled *Study of Young Carers in the Irish Population* (published by the Irish government) examined the phenomena of young carers in the Irish context. The study included interviews with young people and made some policy recommendations. The key finding, based on young people's experiences, was that: '... the quality of informal support networks, formal service provision, the protection of the child's rights and the awareness and recognition of the young carer's caring role greatly influence whether caring has negative or positive impacts for the carer' (p. 93).

As well as identifying the crucial role of social support, the study carefully considered the balance that can be achieved in promoting children's rights and the overall welfare of the family.

Children with mental health problems

There has been an increase in mental health problems amongst children and young people worldwide with figures from the World Health Organisation suggesting 10–20% of all children and adolescents experience a mental disorder currently. There is an increased awareness of such issues for young people, along with recognition of the rising levels of stressors for many young people, which include changes in family structure or the rise of pressures from social media. For some groups of children there are more specific issues of trauma associated with migration journeys or adverse circumstances (Walker, 2013). Recognising the period of change in the life course in adolescence points to the usefulness of a bio-social model to look at intersecting factors (Bailey 2012). Others however, caution against what can be seen as an explosion of diagnosis, particularly of conduct disorders and the difficulty of distinguishing normal behavior from problematic issues (Coppock and Dunn, 2009). Whilst there is no doubt of the increased prevalence amongst children, many urge a focus on combating wider social factors that contribute to mental ill health such as poverty, housing problems and racism.

The Mental Health Foundation charity works across England, Northern Ireland Scotland and Wales, They suggest that up to 1 in 10 suffer and that a large proportion of children with mental health problems are not dealt with early enough. Early intervention especially around psychosis is recommended and there have been some moves around this but also suggestions that it needs to be developed. The *Children and Young People's Mental Health Coalition Report* (2013) had suggested that mental health issues were not receiving enough attention and funding locally. The Young Minds organization is one of the leading charities in the area of young people's mental health in the UK – their recent reports highlight policy recommendations to prioritize mental health and well-being in schools and ensure that appropriate awareness and helpful services are available. Young Minds reported in 2012 that budgets were reduced nationally in the UK, and that the picture of provision, even with regards to age ranges, varied across the country.

There is a clear emphasis now in policy on greater prevention and input, with the UK government policy Children and Young People's Mental Health Taskforce 2015 focusing on early intervention and recommending an increased role for schools. In Scotland the policy review *Children and Young People's Mental Health: A Framework for Promotion, Prevention and Care* found that there is increasing pressure on CAMHs services, but a commitment to early intervention and prevention; this has been followed by the *Mental Health in Scotland – a 10 year vision Mental Health Strategy 2017–2027*. In Wales the Together for Children and Young People Programme (T4CYP) similarly focuses on early intervention; the Children's Commissioner there has drawn up *A Plan for All Children and Young People: 2016–19*, which calls for more timely access to CAMHs and other services. In Northern Ireland higher rates of mental illness prevail in the community. There, a stepped care model is practiced by CAMHs, which includes prevention though family support, primary specialist services (such as for autism or eating disorders) and intensive services (acute or inpatient).

Young people leaving care and aftercare support

There has been widespread recognition that young people brought up in local authority care were often catapulted into independence from care settings, in comparison to their peers and often with very little follow-up. This has led to a range of policy and practice initiatives (Stein, 2012) although the actual provision remains patchy in many areas. The Utting report of 1997 about children in care, *People like Us,* was a landmark publication in terms of the rights of children in care and care leavers. The main principle of changes has been to offer what can be seen as more representative of the assistance which might be offered by a reasonable parent. The introduction of Children (Leaving Care) Act 2000 was an attempt to extend the duties of the local authority to provide a planned transition to independence, with services and financial assistance if required, to those who have been in care (until aged 21 or beyond if in full-time education). The 'Staying Put' policy was recently introduced in the UK in the Children and Families Act 2014, whereby children must be facilitated to stay in foster care after the age of 18 if they wish to: they must also be provided with personal advisers up to the age of 25. Other pieces of legislation do address related areas such as children in care and fostering; in Northern Ireland the Children (Leaving Care) Regulations (Northern Ireland) 2005 and Act 2002, in Scotland the Children and Young People (Scotland) Act 2014 links with the policy 'Getting it right for looked after children and young people'.

Whilst there have been developments in policy and practice for this group of young people, a number of challenges remain for those moving into independence. Brady (2014) points out in a study for Barnardos some of the shortfalls in service co-ordination and the crucial role that support plays for the young people. The care leaver's foundation as a leading charity is taking a role in raising awareness and public perceptions. It has produced a 'Charter for care leavers' which local authorities are asked to sign up to; the charter provides a set of principles to inform all organisations. The website link is below and also features a section on Ireland: http://www.thecareleaversfoundation.org/.

Key point

A report from Barnardos (Glover, 2009) found that building resilience through stability, positive identity and positive educational experiences were important factors for vulnerable children. Resilience has come to be seen a crucial ingredient for young people leaving care and coping with independence, therefore it is the focus of many services in this area.

International examples

Lonne, Parton and Harries (2008) provided a very useful exploration that highlighted the adversarial nature of the child protection system in the UK. Such systems are in place in many countries including Australia and the US and are characterized by an emphasis on bureaucracy and risk management.

By way of a European comparison, a number of countries have a different orientation, for example, the greater family orientation of some of the Latin rim countries, although this can be accompanied by fewer formal supports for families. In other European states a different emphasis is taken through a focus on social pedagogy. A tradition of social pedagogy exists in many countries, where the focus is on a holistic view, a measured approach to risk taking and the use of relationships, partnership and inclusion. The ideas could be usefully translated into the UK practice context.

'Troubled' families

A brief note here on this particular policy seems useful: the projects have been referred to and we know that prior to this, the phenomenon of Intensive Family Support developed in the last few years. The rationale behind this was rooted in the overall movement towards the use of more targeted provision following the 'Families at Risk' Review (2008) in the UK. The Troubled Families initiative developed from Intensive Family Support but differed in terms of taking on more specific aims. These were linked to growing discourses around the rise of the 'underclass' and the concern with antisocial behavior Bristow (2013): the cost benefits of intervention in preventing future problems with certain targeted families were emphasised.

The success of the original projects was evident in various studies and the key worker model appears to be pivotal to the success. Parr (2015) points out the features of such an approach – the key worker and the combination of practical and emotional input. It could be argued that the core of this model, which was originally based on the Dundee project (an Action for children initiative), led to a raft of Family Intervention Projects and were largely successful. The Troubled Families initiative itself, however, has features of stigma and a heavy emphasis on measurable cost outcomes: recent government evaluations of the Troubled Families initiative have brought the model into question even in terms of value for money (Levitas, 2014).

Key tension for reflection: Family support and safeguarding – a focused approach rather than a softer option

There is a continued tension in balancing the provision of support and the protective role of state agencies in most countries – in the UK the balancing of the role of the state has undergone changes over time (Parton, 2014). The roots of child protection itself are of interest here: the historical development of child protection and welfare shows a changing emphasis over time and has often taken a 'child rescue' rather than a family supportive approach (Corby et al., 2012). Important issues and underlying theoretical ideas have emerged, such as a focus on children's rights but also a more recent resurgence in the call for a partnership and strengths-based working with parents. These tensions are also reflected in other countries, where increasingly the emphases on support and strengths are being championed but are difficult to balance with protective functions (Roose et al., 2014).

There are a number of research findings on the experience of parents and children (C4EO, 2010) who are subject to the child protection systems. Although there are positive accounts of this and some good experiences of social work services, the experience of parents tends to be negative on the whole. Lonne et al. (2008) point to the adversarial nature of the child protection system as experienced by many parents. Indeed, some argue that the core tension between an investigative child protection focus versus a broader more supportive approach that has existed in legislation and policy is not resolved (Stafford et al., 2011), and that the tensions continue today in our attempts to work in partnership with families.

There are implications for this negative experience: in most cases the co-operation of parents enhances the outcomes for a child, for example working cooperatively with the agencies can result in the actions of a child protection plan being successful. Indeed there is much recent literature on the importance of relationship building in child protection and welfare. In this way it can be seen that there are benefits to adopting a family supportive approach across the spectrum; it is a focused method rather than a softer option, with the aim of rebalancing through an empowering and supportive emphasis, to actively promote and improve child and family welfare.

Further reading

Fives, A., Kennan, D., Canavan, J., Brady, B. & Cairns, D., 2010. Study of young carers in the Irish population. *The National Children's Strategy Research Services.*

This report provides findings that are more widely applicable, based on consultation with young people.

Grasping the Nettle: Early Intervention for Children, Families and Communities. Available at: http://www.c4eo.org.uk/themes/earlyintervention/files/ early_intervention_grasping_the_nettle_full_report.pdf.
This report on early intervention from C4EO features some 'key messages' for practice.

Seligman, M. & Darling, R.B., 2017. *Ordinary Families, Special Children: A Systems Approach to Childhood Disability.* Guilford Publications.
A well-known and useful textbook about children with a disability.

The care leavers foundation website, available at: http://www. thecareleaversfoundation.org/. Young minds website, available at: https://youngminds.org.uk/.
These are two useful websites with key information and details of services.

5

Family Support Practice and Adult Services

Family support principles applied to adults have been woven through the book in considering how they impact on individuals and families generally. In relation to specific services for adults, some different areas will be outlined, with a focus on how supportive interventions and approaches are relevant. Analysing the underpinning ethos and practice with vulnerable adults highlights some of the issues here and provides the potential for applicability to other service areas.

Additionally, a key emerging area that links to prevention is considered. The overall focus is to explore some of the application of family support principles and approaches across different areas. The chapter will cover:

➤ Working with older people

➤ Homeless services

➤ Adults and mental health

➤ Adverse Childhood Experiences (ACEs) – Links for prevention

➤ *Key tension for reflection: Support and dependency*

Working with older people

This is a key area of work with adults, although as some point out it can be a less valued area (Perry, 2009) and often receives a lower profile than work with children and other groups. It is notable for example that there is much less written in social work texts (Kerr et al., 2005) and many advocate for the role of qualified social work in relation to older people (see Milne et al., 2014). Policy discussions around older people's health and social care have developed due to the population and demographic changes seen across all western countries. The proportion of older adults in the population and the old age dependency ratio are set to increase further in coming decades through longer life expectancy. Whilst the number of older adults (over 65 years) has risen to a figure of around 11.8 million in the UK (Age UK), the numbers over 80 years and 90 years are rising: the number of UK residents 90 years and over has tripled since 1983 (ONS). The picture is similar for other developed countries but conversely, lower life expectancy remains an issue for other countries.

The main policy driver of older people's services over recent years is the integration of health and social care in localities. There had been a general move to shift from more costly acute services to community care in most countries: essentially, a more preventative approach. In the UK, the NHS & Community Care Act 1990 had seen the introduction of the ideas of care management and more efficient multi-agency care packages (Coulshed and Orme, 2012). However, the emphasis of the purchaser–provider split that this heralded was the move to a consumerist market and the viewing of 'care' as a commodity (Galpin and Bates, 2009). These developments also introduced layers of administrative procedure and bureaucracy to services at the expense of direct contact (Lymbery, 2005). The Care Act 2014 in England is the law outlining the care people can expect and it sets out a clear framework for how all parts of the system should protect adults at risk of abuse or neglect. In order to balance choice, dignity and risk a social justice perspective can be taken (Elmer, 2017). Within this legislation, carers are seen as important; there is a focus on eligibility criteria, meeting needs, prevention and safeguarding, with individual *well-being* as the guiding principle. In Wales an integrative piece of legislation now covers care and caring in the Social Services and Well-being (Wales) Act 2014.

Underpinning the services in this area are principles of choice and control with personalisation providing the principle throughout the UK, although the different countries translate this into their own legislation. An ecological lens runs through the assessment processes based on this person-centred approach. However, there is criticism of this in terms of direct payments for older people and the level of resources for social and health care restricting choice in practice (Lymbery, 2005). In terms of needs of older adults, physical health problems are an important area and in meeting need here both medical and social intervention can be required, such as adaptations in the home following hospital discharge, highlighting the need for multi-agency service responses. The rise in people with the syndrome of dementia and associated conditions has led to policy responses such as the 'Living Well with Dementia' strategy (2010) in England and Scotland's more well-developed third 'National

Dementia Strategy' (2017–2020). Given the estimates that there will be an increase to 1.4 million with dementia in the next 30 years, this is a growing area that requires a holistic response for individuals and their carers and families. Many organisations are adopting 'dementia friendly' approaches which is a useful community level response to these changes. The aim is to increase awareness amongst communities and ensure better access to services, a useful example of building community assets.

Viewing the needs of older people through an ecological lens is crucial to see the intersection of factors. The National Institute for Clinical Excellence (NICE) guidelines emphasise the value of social support and networks. Social support can be particularly crucial in later life when people may have reduced networks due to bereavement and other losses of spouses, family or friends. Owing to poor health and mobility, social contact can decrease for some. There is a key role for social support in terms of tackling loneliness and isolation: Age UK estimates that around 1 million will go a month without contact with a family, friend or neighbour. The NHS suggests that loneliness is linked with poor physical and mental health and can lead to depression.

Key point

In later life, the role of social support as a protective factor for physical and psychological health can become more important, in providing a buffer against loneliness and isolation.

Perry (2009) points out fragmentation of categories of older age, with so-called third age people more active and participatory and fourth age older people (with significant physical and health problems) more isolated. Smeaton (2009) looked at people over 80 years and noted their often poorer health, which combined with other factors to increase isolation, finding that even those in shared living arrangements could feel isolated if closeness of relationships was not developed. She suggests that a range of 'low level' activities, including outreach to those who are more socially excluded, is potentially beneficial. Such inputs could help to increase self-esteem: Grembowski et al. (1993) found that the quality of self-efficacy had the effect of lowering health risk behaviour in older people and promoted better health.

> **Key point**
>
> Linking to the theoretical frameworks outlined in Chapter 3, aspects of both social support and an ecological perspective can be useful. Considering protective factors – the development of activities and multiple roles for older people – can add to their sense of self-esteem and self-efficacy.

The value of preventative services in promoting independence and reducing the need for more formal services is important. In a report for the *Scottish Executive Social Research*, Kerr et al. (2005) found the importance of lower level input such as help with household tasks and gardening. Interestingly, it was found that older people particularly valued this type of input that was not just about their physical care, but encompassed wider, quality of life aspects.

Elder stereotypes and discrimination have an effect on social opportunities and older people's own identity and sense of self. Ageist assumptions can be widely held, with an emphasis on loss and decline in later life (Perry, 2009). Older people's needs can also become medicalised rather than seeing the holistic person. Disengagement theory has been used in the past to explain older people withdrawing from society and social activity and contacts. Hall (2012) suggests that it is more useful to look at promoting activity for older people. In recent decades, it could be argued that fixed patterns of behaviour and expectations across the life course have changed, with a blurring of the boundaries of later life, and many people having much more active lives as they age (Levin, 2013). The intersection of various factors can produce additional challenges for ethnic minority older people. Discrimination and disadvantage can accumulate over the life course based on people's socio-economic status (Bécares, 2013), for example greater levels of poverty affecting health or higher levels of manual or lower paid work taking a toll on physical abilities and health in later life.

> **Messages from Research**
>
> Addis et al. (2009) carried out a literature review to explore the social care, health and housing needs for the older LGBT community on behalf of the Welsh Government. Although locating quite limited literature in this area, their findings indicated there ▶

◀

can be a complex picture including isolation and mixed findings that different health behaviours were influencing factors.

A key finding that informs their discussion is the evidence of discrimination and lower take-up of services, with a lack of awareness by services of the existence and needs of the older LGBT community and a reluctance on the part of older people to disclose or discuss their needs.

This suggests the need for further research and consideration by services in this area as the LGBT + elder population increases.

Poverty is a growing issue for older people, with campaigning groups such as Age UK outlining that pensioner poverty affects 1.9 million people in the UK. Alongside income, fuel poverty is a particular issue for older people who are susceptible to falling temperatures; this can be exacerbated by poor housing. The Poverty and Social Exclusion website (part of the ESRC poverty research project) outlines the rise in winter deaths in recent years, particularly amongst the over-75-years group. Poverty of course can exacerbate issues like isolation and will add to stress for individuals. People may have decreased opportunities to take part in social activities due to cost and limited transportation.

Key point

In a changing social and economic context, where active citizenship is increasingly linked with paid work, issues of economic and social isolation for older people are important considerations.

Practice focus

In considering the support needs of older adults, befriending projects can provide much needed contact to reduce social isolation. Smeaton (2009) suggests that such schemes should be further developed, given the multiple benefits of social support and contacts.

Carr and Gunderson (2016) point out some of the benefits of intergenerational contact for both older and younger people. In an informal sense, the best example here is

▶

◄

the grandparent role which occurs within families. More formal arrangements through projects can be made, which draw on utilising the life experience and resources of older people.

Intergenerational projects can increase social contact. They can also provide an additional role for older people, in passing on experiences to younger groups and giving advice. Example of such projects can be found at: https://bit.ly/2xThrsZ.

Homeless services

Seeing homelessness as a human rights issue is advocated by researchers and practitioners in the sector (FEANTSA, 2008; Fitzpatrick and Watts, 2010). In terms of addressing the rights and needs of homeless people, developments based on a largely preventative basis in the sector in the UK countries have been positive. The preventative measures however are set in a context of a reduced supply in housing in many countries, affordability issues, a lack of focus on social housing, and reduced funding to homeless shelters (Just Fair, 2014). The charity consortium Just Fair in the UK argue that the current position on housing and homelessness represents a 'crisis' (ibid) in terms of the people's rights to housing in England. In Ireland, the charity and campaigning group Focus Ireland has been instrumental in highlighting the issues there, where several tragic cases have received recent media coverage. In terms of policy responses to the needs of homeless adults, the consensus on the needs of those who are homeless is a welfare approach and focus on the full range of psychosocial needs (Maeseele et al., 2013). Individuals need to receive practical and financial help initially, and to draw on social support, so that they are able to maintain housing stability in the medium to long term.

Key point

The different types of social support are essential for adults experiencing homelessness. At a basic level, their practical needs for shelter, food, warmth and clothing are required as concrete assistance. Due to individual circumstances, overcoming a sense of stigma, self-esteem and self-efficacy will need to be bolstered, along with social support networks for the future.

There has been a shift in discourse away from a focus on the structural causes of homelessness (Hackworth, 2010), with the emphasis on risk and blame that is characteristic of neoliberal societies (O'Sullivan and Evangelista, 2013). Globally there is a more precarious labour market and a dwindling supply of affordable housing in many countries, clearly leaving some more vulnerable individuals who fall between the gaps. In many cities in Europe, the criminalisation of street homelessness is increasing (Evangelista and Jones, 2013) and there is evidence that particular groups such as migrants are differentially treated in a number of countries.

Defining homelessness reveals the complexity of the area which includes rough sleepers (Teater, 2014), those in hostels/temporary accommodation, and a number of hidden homeless who may be 'sofa surfing' or staying with friends or relatives. Those most likely to experience homelessness include young people, lone parents and those on low incomes or unemployed (Quinney, 2006). Housing and homeless policies tend to target 'priority needs': this can result in some groups receiving less attention from services, such as single homeless people with more complex needs and 'entrenched' rough sleepers. This focus has been reflected in national policy in England which stipulates categories of priority housing need; this idea has dominated policy in the UK since early legislation in the 1970s with a focus on families with children and 'vulnerable' adults (Fitzpatrick et al., 2012). With street homelessness in particular, there are single homeless who do not fall into the priority needs categories outlined in the legislation or those who fall in the grey area of being deemed 'vulnerable', with eligibility for service decided at the local level (Dwyer et al., 2015). In a change to previous funding regimes, resources to target homelessness generally and also rough sleeping had been made available by the New Labour government from the late 1990s in a sector that had previously been neglected. The benefits of this renewed policy approach were felt across the sector, but the new investment had restrictions on whom services could and could not admit, with controls and surveillance such as the local connection rule (Dwyer et al., 2015). In particular the grading of vulnerability in the criteria was bemoaned by those in the sector who wanted to help any homeless person in need, rather than deal with the division between the 'deserving and undeserving homeless' (Bowpitt et al., 2013). Here there are also implications of viewing the 'rough sleeper' population as homogenous, whereas in reality people have varying degree of needs and backgrounds.

There is a renewed focus on the homeless sector as the number of new referrals to services is increasing, along with recognition of the damaging and costly effects of homelessness. However, policy tends to favour those with fewer needs who are able to reform and reintegrate more quickly.

Cornes et al. (2012) noted this in their analysis of the needs of multiple exclusion homelessness, where the causes create 'deep exclusion' and require a policy response that recognises this.

Key point

Taking an ecological perspective can assist in understanding and supporting those with multiple and complex problems, where a variety of life events, possibly addiction or dependency and mental health problems, intersect with their homeless issues.

Practice focus

Peer support

FEANTSA is the European Federation of National Organisations working with the homeless: a policy paper from the group titled *Peer Support: A Tool for Recovery in Homelessness Services* looks at the idea of peer help. This is an idea that has become widely used in a number of service areas, such as in the substance misuse field. One of the key principles is that people who have experienced the issues themselves are in a good position to provide advice and assistance. As discussed in Chapter 3 there can also be reciprocal benefits for the supporter. As an extension of this, former users of services can also go on to more formal roles as paid workers in services.

International example – Housing first

The implementation of variants of the *housing first* approach is a feature of many countries, in comparison to its limited application in the UK. This perspective sees basic shelter needs and permanent housing as the basis for people who can then, with support, work on other issues such as their employment, addiction issues, health and lifestyle changes. The more traditional methods were about treating addiction, mental health and other problems before helping adults into stable housing. There is much evidence to show the longer term success of housing first approaches, with an overview of its potential to be used as part of services in the UK outlined by Bretherington and Pleace (2015) in their review of a number of local services, available at: www.changing-lives.org.uk.

Adults and mental health

The importance of mental health problems worldwide has led the world health organisation to develop a mental health action plan, with the emphasis on issues across the whole life course (World Health Organisation). Positive mental health is being highlighted through public awareness campaigns such as mental health awareness week in the UK. In terms of the complex and diverse nature of mental illness, it includes a whole spectrum of mood disorders, depression, psychosis and schizophrenia as well as organic conditions such as dementia. Particular groups may be more vulnerable based on their experiences such as childhood trauma or social isolation (Glasby and Tew, 2015). It is estimated from surveys that in terms of prevalence, 17% of adults reported they had a common mental health problem within the last week in the UK (Department of Health and Social Care, 2017). The Mental Health Foundation charity, which works across England, Northern Ireland, Scotland and Wales, suggests that 74% of people have at some point felt so stressed that they felt overwhelmed or unable to cope.

There is an emphasis now in policy on greater prevention and earlier intervention. The *No Health without Mental Health* (2011) and the subsequent *Five Year Forward View for Mental Health* (2016) in England and *Towards a Mentally Flourishing Scotland* (2011) suggest more proactive definitions focussing on broader health issues that include mental health as a key aspect (alongside the core legislative framework of the Mental Health Act 1983 and Mental Capacity Act 2005). Although the drivers for community-based services and the care programme approach with a key worker have remained central, the reorganisation of the NHS and modernisation agenda of governments have affected the delivery of mental health services (Glasby and Tew, 2015). In 2015 funding for services was estimated to have been cut by over 8% in real terms despite increased referrals to community and in-patient teams (MIND). Additionally, the smaller voluntary and community sectors, which are an important provider of commissioned services, may experience difficulties in the financial climate (Curry et al., 2011). There is a lack of services at an early or preventative stage for parents with mental health or substance misuse issues (Sawyer and Burton, 2016).

Throughout both primary and secondary mental health services, the medical model tends to dominate even with multi-agency input (Martin, 2014). Looking at the history of mental health services, it is important to emphasise human rights-based approaches and the progress made in terms of user perspectives being acknowledged (Coppock and Dunn,

2009). A recognition of the intersection of medical and social perspectives helps to highlight the complexity of mental illness and the different factors involved, including the effects of discrimination and stigma (Golightley, 2011). A more holistic perspective is useful as it enables the effects of family history to be seen along with environmental factors such as social exclusion, poverty and stress. There are clear links between mental health service users and poverty (Coppock and Dunn, 2009). The Mental Health Foundation charity has produced a *Health Inequalities Manifesto* this year, showing that material and social inequality are key factors in poor mental health depression and lower well-being (Mental Health Foundation, 2018).

Key point

From a family support perspective, looking at a person's social ecology can be helpful in terms of a recovery approach, where a holistic view of health overall is taken. The protective factors of relationships and networks can be harnessed to promote longer term recovery and coping (Golightley, 2011).

Spotlight on disability issues

Disability itself is defined under the Equality Act 2010 and covers a wide range of issues, including physical and sensory disabilities. The disability rights movement had really focussed on empowerment, challenging discrimination, independent living and changes to create more inclusive social and organisational spaces. Services in this area have user involvement and personalised approaches as the norm. Support needs and carers needs tend to be person centered in their ethos although the choice offered by more marketized provision may be limited in practice (Evans, 2014).

However, it is estimated in a report from the Joseph Rowntree Foundation that one-half of adults living in poverty now are disabled or live with a disabled person (Tinson et al., 2016) and from 2012–13 onwards, poverty rates for disabled people have risen in all four UK nations (Joseph Rowntree Foundation). The Disability Rights UK group (2016) has additionally focussed on a lack of economic inclusion, restricted employment opportunities and the burden of affordability of goods and services. Cutbacks in services due to austerity and changes to benefits have led to detrimental effects for disabled people in particular (Oliver, 2013).

Adverse childhood experiences (ACEs) – Links for prevention

There has been an increasing research interest in ACEs owing to the prevalence of adult service users in mental health, health, substance misuse and other services who have experienced such adversity. It is thought that increased vulnerability can stem from these factors: an extensive research body now exists that began in the US. Researchers there were particularly interested in interpersonal violence, community level factors and people's vulnerability to becoming victims, finding that there were associations with:

➤ risky health behaviours,

➤ poor health outcomes and chronic health conditions,

➤ reduced life opportunities, and

➤ mortality rates.

(Adapted from the Centers for Disease Control and Prevention)

Areas that are commonly included as stressors are abuse and neglect and household factors, such as family member in prison, substance misuse or domestic violence. The *Welsh Adverse Childhood Experiences (ACE) Study* was carried out in 2015 on behalf of Public Health Wales (Ashton et al., 2015).

Using questionnaires with adults, they found that 47% of the adults involved had suffered one ACE out of the nine they identified. These covered experiencing sexual, physical or verbal abuse and family factors such as prison, substance misuse, domestic abuse, mental illness, and separation. Key findings were that those with four ACEs or more were three times more likely to suffer heart or respiratory health problems and four times as likely to become diabetic. This suggests that the financial cost to services and the implications for the person are potentially significant. The study recommends investment in both awareness and resources to address and reduce the consequences for individuals. Other studies have pointed to the incidence of offending behaviour based on childhood risks and the preventative approaches that can be taken (Farrington, 2007) and the multiple and longstanding issues for some families known to children's services (Devaney, 2008).

It is important to consider here that many people may have experiences in one of the categories detailed above and we must be careful not to 'pathologise' people's experiences, particularly as they will be mediated by other factors. Additionally it can be argued the focus should be on resilience and recovery rather than an assumption of poor outcomes.

Key point

A key message here from a family support perspective is to increase social supports and resilience for those who have experienced childhood adversity and stressors. Awareness of these factors can open the possibility of both prevention at an individual and community level and also the imperative to provide support and build resilience for individuals.

Key tension for reflection: Support and dependency

In taking a family support stance with adults, the issue of potentially creating dependency can arise. There is much written about the importance of maintaining boundaries and professionalism as practitioners. However, workers often deal with intimate disclosures about previous experiences, emotional issues or mental health: this can often be in the private sphere of someone's home. They will also be dealing with many isolated and vulnerable service users who have multiple needs. Maintaining a balance between relationship building and support can be explored through supervision.

It is suggested that reliance on others for support is best when there is a healthy balance of interdependence and the support is perceived as being available when it will be needed (see Feeney and Collins, 2015). What is crucial here is trying to build sustainable supports, recognising the longer term issues, and the fact that as workers we are only part of a family or individual's world. Facilitating people to build resilience and bolstering their informal social support networks is a core aim of family approaches.

Further reading

Alzheimers Society. Available at: https://www.alzheimers.org.uk/info/20079/dementia_friendly_communities.
This website from the leading charity organisation provides a useful and timely focus for looking at dementia issues across the community.

An evaluation of the Standing Together project. Available at: https://www.mentalhealth.org.uk/publications/evaluation-standing-together-project.
Available on the 'Mental Health Foundation' website, this provides an overview of a proactive peer-support approach to promote mental well-being.

Ashton, K., Bellis, M., Davies, H.K. & Hughes, K., 2015. *Welsh Adverse Childhood Experiences (ACE) Study.* Public Health Wales
Key emerging data on the effects of ACEs from Wales.

Bretherington, J. & Pleace, N., 2015. *Housing First in England.* Available at: www.changing-lives.org.uk.
An exploration of the application of a housing first approach is provided here and is available at the weblink provided.

Jarvis, P., *Adverse Childhood Experiences too High? Educating Yorkshire in ACEs awareness.* Available at: http://www.leedstrinity.ac.uk/blogs/Adverse-Childhood-Experiences-too-High.
This online blog provides a discussion and references on the current debate around ACEs.

PART 3

Working with Diversity and
Inter-Professional Issues

6

Working with Diversity

In this chapter, key issues and practice links will be explored in relation to diversity. The importance of this area in terms of understanding and engaging with service users from a variety of backgrounds is the focus. There are issues that face those who are refugees/asylum seekers or particular communities and these will be explored in the current policy and practice framework. Some of the complex adult and child safeguarding issues that have recently been in the spotlight will be examined.

The emphasis is on links with some of the family support principles that can provide a useful lens on the issues raised. The chapter provides sections that cover:

➢ An overview of culture and ethnicity

➢ Cultural competence

➢ Safeguarding issues

➢ Gypsy, Roma and Traveller families

➢ Asylum seekers/refugees

➢ *Key tension for reflection: Safeguarding issues*

An overview of culture and ethnicity

Diversity as a term can have positive connotations, with the notion of different groups adding to the make-up of society and community (see Thompson, 2011). This idea is closely linked with equality and a socially just approach that counters discrimination. In terms of cultural diversity, 'culture' itself refers to sets of shared social meanings between people that is linked with a common identity. The characteristics of various cultures globally are that they provide a view of the world and guidelines for living and behavior in relation to others that are learned and transmitted between people. Ethnicity refers to a social group that individuals self-identify or are identified by others as belonging to. It includes culture, but other aspects can be included such as language, religion or ancestry (Scottish Public Health). Some essential characteristics necessary to determine an ethnic group were suggested by Lord Frazer in a landmark UK legal case in 1983:

➤ Having a long shared history/memory of which the group is conscious as distinguishing it from other groups; and

➤ Having a cultural tradition, including family, social customs and manners which may be associated with religion.

(Adapted from Bhamra, 2016)

Ethnicity affects most areas of life including employment and family life: it remains a key determinant of socioeconomic status (Hill, 2006). This has an impact for families in terms of not only their income and educational levels but also on health and well-being, which are linked to low socioeconomic status. The intersectionality at play through multifactors can be seen here, showing the importance of taking macro factors from an ecological perspective into account. In terms of potential supports, some studies show the advantages of employment availability for some within ethnic groups and the potentially positive effect of social networks and bonding social capital within groups (Sanders, 2002).

Multiculturalism has been a long established aim in Western countries, however the emphasis on policy in recent years is more on integration and community cohesion (Singh, 2013). Whilst respect and recognition of different cultural and ethnic groups continues, there is an emphasis on citizenship and accepting shared values of a host country. In terms of acculturation or blending in with the existing culture of a country, external factors have influenced how much of original cultural practices are retained by families and how much they might integrate into the 'mainstream' (Sanders, 2002), which can vary with second and third generations and indicates the importance of an approach that takes into account the wider social ecology of families. Criticisms of multiculturalist approaches have developed apart from policy shifts and these emphasise the continued importance and relevance of anti-racist practice in social work and social care services (Bartoli, 2013). A clear anti-racist perspective is required, it is argued, due to the continued disadvantage and poorer outcomes experienced by black and ethnic minority groups (Bhatti-Sinclair, 2011). Multiculturalism and the rise of the role of religion in policy, seen by recent governments as part of building social capital, is also complex in terms of how it fits with other progressive rights (Singh and Cowden, 2011).

The complexity of the issues of identity, ethnicity and 'race' in an increasingly globalised world is influenced by political and historical factors. Press coverage and often intense public debate have renewed on issues around the movement of people, immigration and borders, seen in the refugee 'crisis' in Europe and the EU Referendum in the UK. The England and Wales Citizenship Survey from 2007 found that a majority of all respondents felt that a sense of belonging to Britain and maintaining their own religious identity was possible. In terms of cohesion, the Community Life Survey in England and Wales (2015–16) found more recently that a higher proportion of people (89%) agreed their local area was a place where people from different backgrounds 'get on well together' (Cabinet Office, 2016). A complex picture has recently emerged, however: O'Neill's (2017) report for the Home Office (England and Wales) shows an increase of 29% in hate crimes from the 2015–16 period. This is partly attributable to improved police recording, but also notes increases since the referendum and the Westminster terror attack, with 78% of the hate crime being linked to race hate. In particular, there is a concern that Muslims are viewed as being 'the other,' in contrast to the norm of the majority: a recent report from the Social Mobility Commission (Stevenson et al., 2017) suggested that barriers such as Islamophobia, discrimination and racism are facing many and that 'Muslims experience the greatest economic disadvantages of any faith group in UK society.'

Key point

In some current discourse the ideas of ethnicity and culture have become equated with the issue of immigration. Increased public debate and headlines about immigration also affect groups of people who were born in the UK (The Runnymede Trust). Similarly, in other countries such as Ireland, where higher immigration is a more recent phenomenon, such issues around culture and diversity have come to the fore (Ulin et al., 2013).

Messages from research

The idea of 'superdiversity' has emerged recently to capture the changing picture of many societies: its definition is emerging but is centered around describing and explaining the varied patterns of movement of people globally and multicultural living that have both increased and become more complex in recent decades (Meissner and Vertovec, 2015).

▶

◄

The term superdiversity recognizes that across the globe, there is a time of unprecedented change, mobility and population complexity. The whole issue of diversity within populations has changed rapidly with an added dimension also to people's lives and relationships which often now have a transnational element.

Superdiversity a relatively new term and is finding its way into policy discussions. It is a contested concept however, with arguments that it is bound up in issues of power and politics (Meissner and Vertovec, 2015), along with critique that as an ethnocentrist western idea it potentially has similar pitfalls to multiculturalism in terms of sidestepping structural issues of racism (Ndhlovu, 2016).

The IRIS research centre at the University of Birmingham is leading in the field of superdiversity in the UK, set within one of the most diverse urban areas of the country.

A link to the IRIS centre where further details can be found is: https://www.birmingham.ac.uk/research/activity/superdiversity-institute/index.aspx.

An interesting example of a recent study from the centre is from Grzymala-Kazlowska (2017), who looked at issues for Polish migrants. She suggests that 'social anchoring' is a more useful idea than integration in the current context in British cities. Although the migrants may benefit from increased economic and employment opportunities in the UK, the importance of their socio-psychological stability through such 'social anchoring' is key. This is an interesting example of how important social networks are, and the development of these in a new geographical and cultural context becomes very significant for the migrants.

Key point

Linking to the theoretical frameworks outlined in Chapter 3, family support approaches focus on the social ecology of a person's life and can be helpful in practice to consider social stress and supports. Arguably social support is very key in relation to the psycho-social factors identified by the study above.

Cultural competence

This can be defined as the sum of skills and knowledge that practitioners should develop in relation to working with a diverse range of people. All workers in a sense have a responsibility in becoming competent at both obtaining and applying knowledge about the people from different backgrounds with whom they come in contact and it is suggested there are different levels leading to proficiency. At its core is an acceptance and respect for all cultures. Cultural competence is an acknowledgement and acceptance of differences and of equal respect for all cultures, including an understanding of how culture shapes our own and others' beliefs (Samantrai, 2004). Without this, either individual workers or services can slip into 'cultural blindness', where services fail to take account of important cultural and ethnic traditions and values. This can particularly be the case with less researched groups, for example, understanding the more collectivist roots of intimacy in the parent–child relationships of the Chinese community (Clayton, 2014). Relationship building and service provision can be undermined in such situations by a lack of understanding but also by assumptions (Tedam, 2013).

Although certainly a step forward from 'cultural blindness' of the past, cultural competence is criticised for not sufficiently acknowledging the structural issues and institutional racism that affect people (Abrams and Moio, 2009). Critical race theory, an alternative perspective originating in the US, focusses on the continued structural inequality that exists throughout societal structures that reinforce inequality and discrimination (Crofts, 2013). The intersectional experiences of different groups along lines of race, gender and class are acknowledged here. In practice therefore, a preferred approach of *cultural humility* has been suggested (Fisher-Borne et al., 2015). This encourages practitioners and services to challenge barriers, not just to understand the culture and practices of 'others', and also suggests a continued process rather than the end point of achieving cultural competence. Similarly, the idea of 'minoritised communities' rather than ethnic minorities suggests the active social processes that contribute to the position of groups. There is an increasing recognition of the complex picture of how culture and race affect outcomes for the person, service responses and help-seeking behaviour (Kirmayer, 2012) and more generally affect family needs and issues (Bhatti-Sinclair, 2011). In emphasizing both barriers and supportive networks at the individual and community level, a family support perspective can usefully contribute to such perspectives.

International perspective

A study on parents' perception of social support in contexts of diversity was carried out in Belgium by Geens et al. (2017). They were interested in the role of early childhood care settings where increasing support through bonding and bridging social capital to develop social cohesion in urban areas is a policy aim.

▶

◄

The findings suggested that from the parent's perspectives, a complex picture emerged. There were specific effects of parenthood itself on social contacts and isolation, which apply across all parents in different settings and countries. Along with this, some of the effects of the mixed urban area which included lack of social supports was felt. They concluded that although a varied picture emerged, with less development of cohesion, so-called 'lighter' encounters parents had with others through attending the setting were thought to be of value.

The study showed that, although increasing integration and community cohesion was the desired policy outcome, from parents' perspectives, the brief social contact with others was a benefit in itself.

Safeguarding issues

Reference to several high profile cases highlights the difficult line some-times encountered between respecting cultural norms and recognizing abuse. It is important to be aware of differences in child rearing practices such as attitudes to discipline and punishment (Robinson, 2007) and also to avoid stereotyping or assumptions that contributes to the overrepre-sentation of groups in child welfare systems (Stokes and Schmidt, 2011). However, belief systems can impact on both adult and child protection, with the need to respond to abusive practices.

Faith-based abuse can take different forms but is rooted in belief sys-tems that attribute behaviours or characteristics to particular factors. There can be an assumption that an evil being is controlling an adult or child through spirit possession or that a person is able to perform evil acts through witchcraft powers. In these circumstances techniques of exor-cism to expel the evil source can be carried out, which can lead in some instances to physical harm and abuse. Additionally, for children there is also the potential of emotional harm through being labelled. In terms of policy, the 'Child abuse linked to faith or belief, National Action Plan 2012' has been drawn up in the UK. The importance of these issues was highlighted in particular with the Victoria Climbie case. Bartholomew (2015) welcomes the international attention on this issue and outlines some of the reasons for such practices and the relationship with long-held beliefs from countries of origin which can be complex and sometimes linked to the legacy of macro or political issues.

Awareness of female genital mutilation (FGM) has increased with a renewed focus on legislation and media campaigns. The practice is responsible for a range of short- and long-term medical effects as well as trauma, emotional and psychological effects for women, children and young people. FGM is illegal in all counties of the UK with the Female Genital Mutilation Act 2003 amended by the 2015 Serious Crime Act to include FGM Protection orders (for Scotland, the Prohibition of Female Genital Mutilation Act 2005) and is specifically included in the most recent safeguarding guidance. Despite this, to date there have been no convictions in the UK, although it is estimated 137,000 women and girls are affected in England and Wales (NSPCC). Important here is the idea of working with communities, taking a clear stance against the practice and developing an understanding about the deep-rooted nature of the associated traditions and beliefs. Practical guidance on agency responsibility, a focus on prevention, and also support for affected women are seen as key (Khalifa and Brown, 2016). An example of a successful peer education programme is the NESTAC health initiative which makes use of community youth advocates and peer support; further information is available at: http://www.nestac.org/Nestac/ourprojects.html.

Key point

Prevention work on such issues through building community awareness and advocacy schemes is vital, coupled with multi-agency awareness of the signs and taking a robust approach. Social support built through counselling and emotional support are important for those affected.

Gypsy, Roma and Traveller families

Through the Equality Act 2010 which defines protected characteristics, both Gypsies and Irish and Scottish Travellers can constitute an ethnic group. Gypsy Roma and Traveller peoples now live across most parts of the UK and Ireland.

Travellers have a distinctive lifestyle and culture; Irish Travellers have been documented as having a long history and Roma peoples have their own nomadic history, traditions and language, being Europe's largest minority ethnic group (Pavee Point).

As communities, they can suffer deprivation across a number of areas. Health outcomes are poorer with higher mortality and child mortality rates. A history of experiencing prejudice can lead to a mistrust of outside agencies, contributing to health issues (Van Cleemput, 2010). In terms of education, 'Traveller pupils are still the group most at risk in the education system. They are the one minority ethnic group which is too often "out of sight and out of mind"' (Ofsted, 2003). Having an inclusive ethos within a school that considers parent and wider community relations as well as the specific service provided by the Traveller education service can help here (Bhopal and Myers, 2009).

Discrimination and racism exist and affect families, communities and children: 'Discrimination against Gypsies and Travellers appears to be the last "respectable" form of racism' (Philips, 2004). Nearly 9 out of every 10 children and young people from a Gypsy background have suffered racial abuse and nearly two-thirds have also been bullied or physically attacked (Ureche and Franks, 2007). They can also be affected by negative or sensationalist press coverage (see Clark, 2015). From a family support perspective this societal context and the experiences of families produces additional challenges and it is also important to recognize the strengths and resilience of communities. The Pavee Point Traveller and Roma Centre website is produced by this organization (based in Dublin) and provides a range of useful information and resources including factsheets – Available at: http://www.paveepoint.ie/.

Key point

Intersectional disadvantage experienced by such communities can be better understood from a social justice perspective. Awareness of disadvantage, racism experienced and reduced opportunities and inequality point to the importance of looking at all parts of the social ecology.

Asylum seekers/refugees

In terms of definitions, separated children or unaccompanied minors are those under the age of 18 years old who are outside their country of origin and separated from either parents or caregiver (UNHCR). The 1951 United Nations Convention on Refugees states that a refugee is a person outside his or her own country owing to a well-founded fear of being persecuted for reasons of race, religion, nationality, membership in a particular social group or political opinion (Article 1A (2)). Asylum seekers are defined as those 'who have left their country and are seeking refuge status with Asylum being the protection granted to refugees by a government'. In other terms, a displaced person has left their home in fear but has not crossed an international border and so is an internal refugee, and finally an economic migrant has left their country to find work or a higher standard of living in a new country. The UK receives only about 1% of the world's refugees (UNHCR Global Trends 2015, The Refugee Council) and just 3% of all asylum claims made in the EU so far in 2016 (Eurostat 2016, The Refugee Council).

Financial support for refugees/asylum seekers and access to services varies, with some countries taking a punitive approach with the use of detention centres. In the UK asylum seekers have more limited access to cash benefits which are set at around one-half of mainstream welfare payments and accommodation is provided through dispersal policies. In Ireland the direct provision system has been widely seen as restrictive. The Refugee Action charity estimates that 45% have been unable to buy fresh fruit and vegetables since being in receipt of asylum support. Charities and advocacy groups look to provide emotional and often practical support such as bus passes to travel to appointments provided by the Refugee Survival Trust in Scotland.

From a family support perspective the context of provision produces additional challenges. Typically, people may be lacking in social support networks which can be exacerbated by policies of detention and dispersal. For families, lack of access to money can restrict social networks and activities, with one parent revealing: 'I cannot take them anywhere like museum, or anywhere to play and meet other children. To go out, you need money and we don't have a penny to spare' (Ibid). Asylum seekers/ refugees are seen as a vulnerable group, with higher rates of mental health and health issues from previous trauma (Schouler-Ocak et al., 2016) and the stress of the asylum process itself, which can be drawn out over a long period. A resilience-oriented approach to treatment is a useful stance here (see Laban, 2015).

Key point

In terms of practical help and social and emotional well-being, this is arguably the most crucial area of work with all migrants who will have left at least some key supports behind and will be facing the context of provision and conditions in the host country.

The value of resilience for unaccompanied minors has been referred to in other chapters, in particular the studies by Mels et al. (2008) and Smyth et al. (2015) who explored the importance of social support networks and formal and informal support in different countries. Additionally, the role of faith as a buffer and a source of social support for this group was noted in an Irish study (Ní Raghallaigh and Gilligan, 2010). Given the trauma and stress that young or child migrants may have experienced, factors that can help to build resilience for children and young people are important to consider; these include school support, developing peer networks, access to therapeutic services and activities and achievements.

Key tension for reflection: Safeguarding issues

Bernard and Gupta (2006: 476) refer to some of the pitfalls of cultural pluralism that can exist in child protection services, reflecting views that without a clear perspective: 'On the one hand, a pathologizing approach to black families may lead to unnecessarily coercive intervention and, on the other hand, a cultural relativist approach may lead to non-intervention when services are required'.

In terms of culture and parenting, racism in wider society and institutions and families' experience of discrimination or insensitivity can lead to defensiveness or lack of engagement (Barker and Hodes, 2007). Bhatti-Sinclair and Price (2015), in analyzing serious case reviews, suggest a nuanced, individual and skilled approach to each case rather than assumptions about caring and family roles in different cultures.

The recent joint serious case review on the sexual exploitation of children and vulnerable adults in one English city refers to the issue of culture, influenced by religion, which can lead to complex attitudes about childhood, abuse, vulnerability and different views of the authorities (Spicer, 2018). A report for the Muslim Women's Network UK centres on the more hidden problem of sexual exploitation of Muslim women and girls, which remains largely unreported and where cultural barriers to disclosure and reporting exist (Gohir, 2013).

It can be suggested that family support as a perspective that looks to the intersecting social ecology of individuals and communities provides an opportunity to look at such issues from a social justice perspective.

Suggested reading

Bartholomew, L., 2015. Child abuse linked to beliefs in witchcraft. *Transnational Social Review*, 5(2), pp. 193–198.

This journal article provides an overview of child protection and an aspect of faith-based abuse.

IRiS Research Centre. Available at: https://www.birmingham.ac.uk/research/activity/superdiversity-institute/index.aspx.
Links can be found through this to a range of current research and resources around superdiversity from the University of Birmingham.

Khalifa, S. & Brown, E., 2016. *Communities Tackling FGM in the UK: Best Practice Guide*, the Tackling Female Genital Mutilation Initiative and Options Consultancy Services Limited, London.
This resource is available online and provides a very user friendly approach to the issues, focussed at a community and prevention level.

Pavee Point Traveller and Roma Centre. Available at: http://www.paveepoint.ie/.
The website of the Traveller and Roma community provides information, support and useful background information that can be accessed by communities and practitioners.

7

Multi-Agency Working and Family Support

Collaborative working is a practice imperative in all areas of service provision and it is an essential component of family support practice. Some of the policy context, theoretical background and models of multi-agency working will be explored in terms of how they relate to family support. Partnership and collaboration with children, young people and families is at the heart of family support principles and it is this approach that is of key interest here.

Some of the challenges along with some models of good practice will be identified and the reader can consider these in the light of their own experiences. The overall aim of multi-agency work in enhancing services for both children and adults will be the focus.

➢ Principles of partnership and collaboration: With and for families

➢ Multi-agency working: The policy context

➢ Challenges and barriers

➢ Developments in children's services multi-agency approaches

➢ The workforce: Different roles

➢ *Key tension for reflection: Achieving true partnership with family?*

Principles of partnership and collaboration: with and for families

Collaboration is the process of partnership put into action (Weinstein et al., 2003, in Gasper, 2010). Although widely promoted at both organisational and individual levels, partnership working still produces practical challenges. Team working in any sense requires some input from its members and generally involves planned actions by team members and stakeholders that lead to working together. In current services for individuals and families, cooperative working is increasingly required across agencies but also in less defined 'teams' such as professionals involved in a 'Team around the Child'.

As Frost (2005) has outlined there are a number of terms in this area that suggest increasing levels of collaboration: cooperation between agencies at the lower end, co-ordination, and then integration of services at the most developed end of the spectrum. Many terms are used interchangeably when referring to different agencies or professionals working together namely: interagency, joined-up working, multidisciplinary, multi-agency and partnership working. There is now a wealth of literature on the subject which suggests that there are some common ingredients to 'working together' which include communication, assertive leadership a supportive culture, individual practitioner qualities and organisational elements. For effective interprofessional work to take place therefore, individuals involved need to:

➢ Be motivated to engage with other professionals

➢ Understand the holistic needs of service users

➢ Be competent – secure in own knowledge base and in own role

➢ Have open and honest communication.

➢ Practice trust and mutual respect

➢ Be willing to managing conflict with others (see Larson and LaFasto, 2003)

Key point

From a family support perspective, a range of agencies not only working together in partnership, but working both *for* and *with* families is important. Indeed one of the ten principles of family support outlined by Dolan et al. (2006) emphasises this in Principle One: *'Working in partnership is an integral part of family support. Partnership includes children, families, professionals and communities'*.

Co-location of different agencies and services has become more commonplace. Such arrangements enable shared expertise to be pooled to deal with particular sets of issues. Evaluations of co-located services reveal increased levels of understanding of each role and greater levels of communication, although as Leadbetter et al. (2007) point out, co-location in itself may not lead to co-working, unless good practice around working together in general takes place. In many other cases a 'team' may be loosely defined and may consist of a number of professionals working with an individual or a family who could be described as a 'virtual team'. In some cases such a group may not meet due to time and distance restraints but their input could be co-ordinated by a social worker or key worker. The idea of a 'team around the child/family' in whatever form it takes is useful in another sense in that it reflects the central place that the child and/or family has in relation to services. Considering collaborative working through the lens of family support places the focus firmly on the experiences and effects on individuals and families.

A holistic perspective is at the core of working together, with the different aspects of a child's or family's life and their needs considered. Some of the benefits for service users are increased identification of a range of needs, different resources identified, a focus on empowerment, better actions and more coherence in action plans (Gasper, 2010). The overall benefits of interprofessional working are widely recognised and can be summarised from the literature in the children and family arena as:

➤ Early identification of need and intervention

➤ Better support for parents

➤ Children's needs addressed more appropriately

➤ Better quality services

➤ Reduced need for more specialist services

These are benefits from multi-agency working that really chime with family support practice with its emphasis on meeting needs holistically.

Key point

There are different degrees to which services and professionals collaborate. An issue from a family perspective is ensuring that there is greater clarity about the point of contact for services, rather than having to contact multiple services. This was an important guiding principle of children's disability services in the UK, helping to ensure that families didn't have to repeat their information to different professionals involved in their children's lives: there had been longstanding concerns based on research in this area that families experienced difficulty in navigating the range of services (Sloper et al., 2006).

Multi-agency working: The policy context

The imperative for multi-agency working has been reinforced in most serious case reviews in children's services. Recommendations about multi-agency co-operation featured in the Laming Report (2003) and the subsequent Children Act 2004, and again in the Laming Report (2009), where interagency working was a feature of the conclusions. It has run as a thread throughout all the 'Working Together to Safeguard Children' guidance up to the present version. Multi-agency working and cooperation is much discussed as a feature in terms of the failures to implement this effectively (Reder and Duncan, 2004). Many pinpoint a paradigm shift in moving to joined-up working during the New Labour government in the UK. This was the period when Sure Start centres developed and the language of partnership working really began to spread. Sure Starts often had different specialists from across services providing a holistic assessment and meeting the needs of families (Frost and Robinson, 2007). These features continue in the children's centres model throughout the UK, with the mix of early years services, parenting input, child health, advice or drop-in services (Hall et al., 2015).

An example of a recent policy initiative can be found in Scotland where the government has initiated the 'Realigning Children's Services'. This is intended to influence strategic commissioning decisions. The main aim of the programme is to strengthen partnership working across children's services, as well as an emphasis on research evidence about children's well-being. Details can be found on the website: http://www.gov.scot/Topics/People/Young-People/realigning-childrens-services.

In the adult services arena, collaborative practice has also become a feature of every policy initiative and legislation the last few decades. It has become a dominant underlying principle of legislation particularly with the interface between health and social care; adult safeguarding is built on the ideas of multi-agency cooperation. In terms of such services, increased joined-up working is seen as synonymous with cutting bureaucracy and improving efficiency. Interestingly it could be suggested that the widespread changes and privatisation of service delivery that occurred from the 1980s onwards led to fragmentation and a greater need for a policy and practice response that '...represents a significant reorientation of professional working practices' (Pollard et al., 2005).

Practice focus

One example of a holistic approach to communication and information sharing can be found in the example of the 'Conversations 4 change' that are suggested by Haringey council's Early Help service. In the referral and assessment to early help services, the communication that has taken place with families and between agencies is recorded. This communication focuses on needs and concerns about children and their families, through conversations, where it is felt that some aspects of a child's needs are not being met and additional input may be necessary. The emphasis is on a two-way conversation, particularly with families themselves.

This is seen as a helpful way of considering communication and information sharing within and between agencies. Agencies are strongly encouraged to hold conversations with the family also and to be guided by the principles of promoting child welfare and providing timely intervention.

More information is available on the Haringey council website at: http://www.haringey.gov.uk/children-and-families/early-help.

Messages from research

The LARC studies are a series of evaluations from the Local Authorities Research Consortium, which was set up to promote the development of integrated working in local councils in the UK. Integrated working practices and outcomes for children and families are examined in a series of these LARC research reports. The latest of the studies looks at responses to the identification of neglect and some of the attempts at early intervention around this. The findings recommend the following:

– Promoting existing services, with simpler process and fewer waiting lists

– Improving collaborative working around neglect

– Reducing stigma of referrals and families' knowledge about the help available

– Raising community and practitioner awareness about different levels of neglect

These findings place a clear emphasis on factors that improve the service and raise awareness at the family and community level.

Further information is available at their website: https://www.nfer.ac.uk/larc2-integrated-childrens-services-and-the-caf-process/.

Practice focus

There are many benefits from working *in partnership* with children. In terms of softer outcomes, the benefits are that children can feel listened to. If a child has disclosed issues or concerns they are more likely to feel that these are being acted upon at the child's pace. A partnership orientation can also assist the practitioner in understanding the child's definition of issues and provide some insight into the child's world. Here, relationship building with a child or young person is essential to be able to move towards planning together.

The research forum C4EO published a review and summary of a literature review on children's and young people's views of both child protection services and court proceedings. In relation to young people's experiences and views, the authors found few research studies in this area in the previous decade. In relation to experiences of becoming involved in the child protection 'system', young people found a lack of information was given and they had quite traumatic experiences initially, seeing it as a confusing and not a child-friendly system (C4EO, 2010).The statutory guidance set out in WTSC 2015, similarly to the statutory guidance pertaining to Scotland and Northern Ireland, outlines a child-centred approach that should be taken in all safeguarding and child protective work. The Children Act 1989 had set out the legal requirements to ensure that due regard is given to the child's wishes and obtaining the child's 'wishes and feelings' is an essential part of assessments. This child-centred lens had also been a core feature of Munro's report (2011) and the second interim report (2010) was aptly titled *The Child's Journey*. The voices of children and young people were seen as an important part of Munro's investigation into the child protection system where a summary of children's viewpoints is provided, and this has influenced the statutory guidance. Similarly, the new Ofsted inspection framework in England now has the journey of the child as its focus.

The current resurgence in interest about relationship-based models has focused attention on the engagement of the child and young person by social workers in particular (Winter, 2010). There is arguably a need for a refocus on skills in engaging, working in partnership across the spectrum of child welfare and protection.

Challenges and barriers

There is a good deal of current writing and research on some of the barriers to effective interprofessional working, which continues to provide challenges. Some issues summarised from the literature are:

➢ Lack of confidence about how and when to share information and which information to share

➢ Lack of common guidance on information sharing across services

➤ Communication difficulties

➤ Not knowing who to contact around information sharing

➤ Professional hierarchies

➤ Lack of understanding of different agency roles and responsibilities

➤ Competing or conflicting targets

Gasper (2010) considered some of the complexity of agencies working together in terms of the relationships, perceptions of power and authority, influences of one's own professional training and time or financial pressure. To deal with some of these complexities and issues takes a real commitment from professionals. Additionally, although the benefits of collaborative working have been well established, it can be more time consuming in practice. Barnes (2016 in Davies and Jones) focussed on the distinct identity of each profession, which is highlighted in the language used and their sets of beliefs and values about service users and their issues. Along with these factors and professional hierarchy in organisations, she cites a positive view of multiprofessional working from a study carried out by Hudson (2002). This study suggested that coming together with a clear focus on how to benefit service users can promote good 'working together'. Roets et al. (2014) explored joined-up working, in line with current trends, in two settings in Belgium: they identified that systems can result in functional responses but that there is the potential for different agencies to overlap and take a more considered response to supporting families.

Sharing information is one example of an area of complexity where conflict and uncertainty can arise between agencies. Sections 10 and 11 of the Children Act 2004 in the UK created a gateway for sharing of information between agencies in child welfare. The statutory guidance emphasises how essential information sharing within and between agencies is to safeguarding, however there have been numerous examples from serious case reviews of failures to appropriately do so. A guiding principle is that sharing without consent should be considered on a case by case basis, and if it is in the public interest, with such decisions documented. This is important in family support terms in balancing the rights of the child and ensuring robust safeguarding.

Key point

There are challenges to working with different professionals and with agencies that might have different goals and often a different pace of working. However, Davis et al.

▶

◄

(2012) suggest that the diverse experience of team members can be a real benefit that leads to more creative solutions. It is this focus of ensuring that we consider the best for children and their families that is the driver for practice.

International example

The development of crucial concepts in social work practice with families and communities in Slovenia is captured in an interesting new text: *Co-Creating Processes of Help: Collaboration with Families in the Community* (2016). Čačinovič Vogrinčič's contribution chapter outlines an approach to working collaboratively when assessing and providing support to families, often against a backdrop of poverty and multiple problems in the Slovenian context. The focus is on working towards solutions together and viewing families as 'allies' in the process.

Some of the core principles of family support are applied, with an emphasis on valuing informal and existing social networks and seeking to maximise these. The focus on practical and financial help is crucial particularly in situations of poverty and disadvantage. Interestingly, such input is recognised as being a building block of the overall relationship with the family, promoting a sense of real understanding of the family's situation and fostering a sense of solidarity with the family. Here we see the value of the practical side of family support which has a number of different benefits for the family and, crucially, the family–worker relationship.

The sense of 'working together' meaningfully with the family is a real aim of these services.

Developments in children's services multi-agency approaches

Two examples from the raft of multi-agency developments in children's services are considered here, highlighting both the increase in collaboration between agencies and professionals, along with some of the benefits from the child–family perspective.

The signs of safety approach

The Signs of Safety (SoS) model is a specific approach to child protection and is outlined in Chapter 8 in more detail. At its core the model takes a collaborative focus both between agencies and with families, where strengths and risks are assessed with the involvement of the parents and all agencies involved. Evaluations of SoS child protection meetings have found that professionals are more involved in putting forward their opinions and views (Baginsky et al., 2017). The different agencies and professionals contribute more to discussions and take responsibility for the assessment of risk and the development of plans for children. It has also been noted that families are clearer from the SoS process: they typically have more involvement in the process and an increased understanding (Bunn, 2013), with the roles of different agencies and services available being more clearly explained.

The model shows the benefit of such multi-agency and collaborative working as wider supports are considered for families. Families' relationships with a range of professionals are improved, which can assist in the longer term engagement with services.

MASH teams

Multi Agency Safeguarding Hubs were set up in a number of areas in the UK from 2008 onwards. The prime aim of the hubs was to provide better information sharing and responsiveness to safeguarding across agencies. The hubs consist of staff from agencies including the police, social care and NHS staff who work together in co-located settings. Building trust between the agencies and confidence to share information were seen to be some of the benefits from working so closely together. Careful planning and involving all partners in the planning is seen to be important, given the complexity of sharing information with legislative parameters (IISaM). In Devon county council, an internal evaluation showed increased referrals to early help services after the setting up of the service there. This suggested that a more efficient system of identifying need and early help requirements was operating in the area (C4EO, 2017) due to this interagency setting.

The workforce: different roles

Stone and Rixon (2008) consider the changing landscape of the 'professions' in which identity and boundaries between groups can be more 'fluid' in the context of increased joined-up working. Jones and colleagues (2013, in Davies and Jones, 2015) felt that there was what they described as a 'soup or salad' effect in multiprofessional teams. They saw that different roles either retained their distinct professional identity or on the other hand, become blended or merged with others. Gasper (2010) has pointed out that hierarchies are increasingly less important in children's services – he refers to what can be described as the 'new professional' who is very much open to ideas of multiagency working and is skilled and equipped to carry this work out.

Many of the different roles involved in supporting families are professional with a number who are less qualified, but none the less experienced and skilled staff who can be described as 'paraprofessional'. Arguably, it is important that there is a parity of esteem between workers. Family support roles often focus on direct work and relationship building. As such, they can have a great deal of knowledge and information about the children and families that they work with to contribute to assessments. Often the goals and actions from child protection conferences or from core groups are actioned to the family support worker: increasingly so with the restrained role of direct work for social workers. Frost et al. (2015) articulate a clear argument about the development of the wider workforce, including all levels of staff.

Key point

The different roles in the sector, including volunteer and informal roles, play an important part in intervention. Collaborative and multi-agency working with a family support perspective encourage us to value the contributions of each.

Key tension to reflect on: Achieving true partnership with family?

A tension in family support work is that partnership with families is a key tenet of the work but it is questionable to what extent a true partnership can be achieved through formal services. The aim of support is to empower, but as in the case of statutory social care services, families are required to attend or participate in services. They can be involved in assessments but the decisions ultimately lie with the professional: families may ultimately be seen as a subject of intervention rather than a partner. What is important to the family support approach is an honest and open communication – that families are clear about the role they can take is encouraged, to maximise this. This has been referred to as being a 'relational dance' in implementing a strengths-based model in child protection work (Roose et al., 2014), where practitioners try to balance relationship building and working together with their statutory duties.

McLaughlin (2013) challenges the dominant mantra that interprofessional working is always a positive, as across the spectrum of social care issues, some may in fact be best dealt with by one professional. Principally he points out that the voice of the service user can often become secondary to the professional's agenda: joined-up working can be good when it '... focuses more upon the service user and their views and less upon the process of workers working together' (p. 963). The evidence base from government sources for working collaboratively tends to highlight successes (Quinney and Hafford-Letchfield, 2012), rather than the perspectives of service users across the range of services. It could be said that there is an aspiration for service user partnership but that this is often an 'unrealised vision' (Pollard et al., 2005: 15).

The family support principles (Dolan et al., 2006) in a sense provide a template for family and service user involvement across the spectrum. The current practice landscape is indeed placing new demands on professionals and agencies, but does provide an opportunity to realign focus on the service user as being at the centre. As Edwards (2004) points out, a real focus on children's lives and the wider factors influencing them can be a key benefit from multi-agency working. A clear family support orientation helps to provide this focus within the complexity of current services.

Further reading

Buchanan, E., Poet, H., Sharp, C., Easton, C. & Featherstone, G., 2015. *'Child Neglect is Everyone's Business'. Achieving a Greater Sense of Shared Responsibility for Tackling Neglect: Findings from LARC 6*. Slough: NFER. Available at: https://www.nfer.ac.uk/publications/LRCN01.
This report as part of the study series is available online, with a focus on child neglect in LARC 6.

Frost, N., 2014. Interagency working with children and families: What works and what makes a difference? *Changing Children's Services: Working and Learning Together*, p. 143.
A solid outline of the key issues in interagency working appears in this book chapter.

Mešl, N. & Kodele, T., 2016. *Co-Creating Processes of Help: Collaboration with Families in the Community*. Ljubljana: Faculty of Social Work.
This textbook gives a detailed account and analysis of emerging support services with partnership at their core, in the context of a particular country.

McLaughlin, H., 2013. Motherhood, apple pie and interprofessional practice, *Social Work Education: The International Journal, 32*(7), pp. 956–963.
A critique and analysis of the concepts of interprofessional working are provided in this article, with a particular service user focus.

PART 4

Examining Current Issues and Looking Forward

8

Contemporary Approaches

At the forefront of contemporary practice in the social care field are a number of approaches that share the principles of family support and draw on the use of a strengths-based orientation and empowerment. Some models that have gained recent currency are not necessarily new ideas but are being implemented in the current practice context.

Some of these areas will be outlined in this chapter and their merits analysed. These give readers a chance to focus on up-to-date and innovative areas that are rooted in theory and findings from evaluations, linking well with the current move to ensure that social workers and other professionals enhance their skills throughout the career pathway. This interest in new ways of working comes at a time in when there is a general consensus in the UK and beyond that services should be identifying and implementing best practice in line with recent policy and research.

➤ Intensive support

➤ Restorative practice

➤ Strengths based and solution focussed

➤ Signs of safety

➤ Domestic abuse and violence

➤ Direct work in complex systems

➤ Changing behaviours

Intensive support

Promoting the welfare of vulnerable and complex families through a range of practical and emotional support is a crucial concept for family support. The intensive input that was developed in the family interventions projects (FIPs) in the UK (and similar intensive models elsewhere) has been found through several research studies and evaluations to have positive effects for families (Parr, 2009; Flint et al., 2011). The FIPs were seen in particular to promote improved outcomes for children, young people and their families. Families who are faced with a range of complex and often longstanding issues feel they have been supported through a range of practical and other inputs. Although the successor of the FIPs in England, the Troubled Families projects, were very much tied in with particular government agendas around employment and parental behaviour targets, evidence from the projects does indicate some similar positive results and a continuity of the work carried out by FIPs (Holmes et al., 2015), with the second phase focussing usefully on parental conflict within families. As an earlier discussion pointed out, the newer policy has led to some areas using a different and less stigmatising name for troubled families' projects (Ibid).

One aspect of intensive family interventions is the targeted and multi-agency input: this runs alongside the key worker system where dedicated time from a particular worker is allocated for a period. The practical and emotional support that is the hallmark of these services was praised by the government's troubled families tsar, Louise Casey (2012), as being a no-nonsense, 'sleeves rolled up' initiative that combined practical and supportive elements. The role of the key worker in intensive family support is thought to also enhance the relationship building capacity of the worker with the family, thus helping the success of the intervention (Parr, 2016). Although this relational style of working as part of key working may be seen as a softer and more unfocussed option, Parr (2015) points out that this relational stance is based on a rich set of skills, with the relational aspect *in itself* producing positive effects for the families. A variety of small-scale qualitative studies and evaluations points to particular emotional and psychological benefits experienced by families. Such benefits can promote an increase in self-esteem and self-efficacy; however, these can be viewed as being 'softer' outcomes that are less measurable (Bond-Taylor, 2015).

Key point

The focus now of intensive family support is more on intervention; however, many of the benefits are arguably the 'softer' outcomes which families find supportive and empowering. The key worker is pivotal to this, with a focus on enhancing less tangible qualities like emotional and psychological well-being.

Practice focus

Martina had spoken to a worker at her children's school about severe domestic abuse from her new partner during his bouts of drinking; the school had been supporting Ela, aged 7, and Masie, aged 9, because they were beginning to come to school hungry, often late and with poor hygiene. After consultation with children's social care and an assessment, a child protection case conference had resulted, after which Martina separated from her partner. Martina's family had previously been involved in the child protection system when the children were younger, and after several years of stability, she felt that things were again 'falling apart' as she had little wider family to help her.

The referral to the FIP project was a turning point for Martina. The key worker quickly developed a supportive relationship with Martina, providing practical help and modelling around routines of getting ready for school. The support and encouragement helped Martina feel less overwhelmed, along with input from other agencies including her GP and domestic abuse counselling for all the family. The worker also spent time focussing on the children's views: they were beginning to feel 'different' at school. The main benefit for the family was a sense that they could move forward and overcome the issues. Thinking about their views and their daily lives, what specific benefits to the emotional and psychological well-being of each family member would there be in the longer term if this intervention was successful?

Restorative practice

The underpinning rationale behind restorative practices is the idea that people are more likely to make positive changes when those in positions of authority do things *with* them rather than *to* them or *for* them. This is explained in the 'Social Discipline Window', adapted from Wachtel and McCold (2000), shown below. The table shows that restorative thinking requires a balance of high levels of control and limit setting along with high levels of support and encouragement. This suggests that a high control approach coupled with low support will lead to a more authoritarian stance which is less helpful to service users as it will feel that they are being told to change. On the other hand, taking a more 'hands off' or low control style may appear more empowering at first glance, but if this is accompanied by only low levels of support it becomes neglectful as the persons' needs will not be met.

Four ways of being

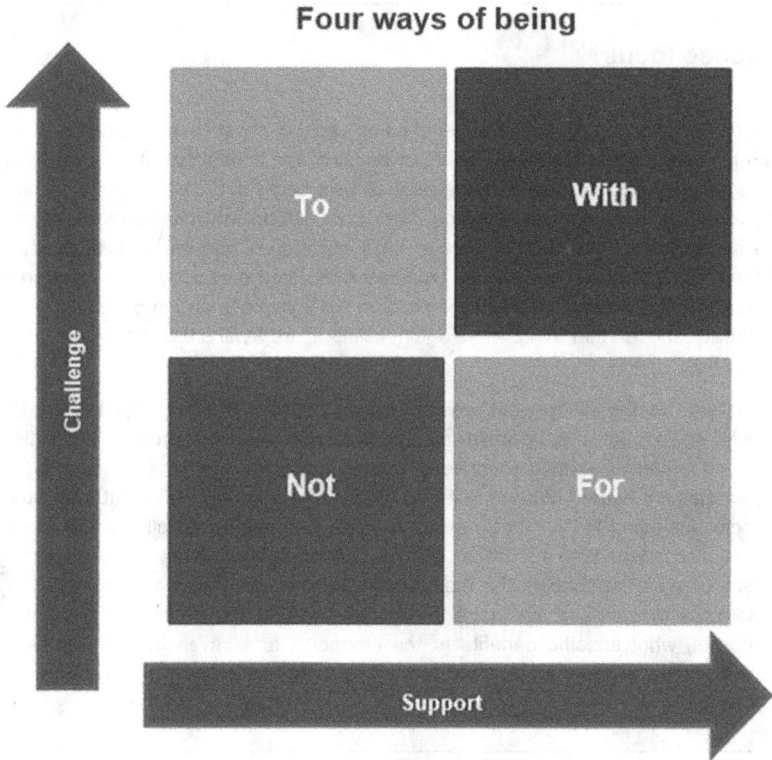

Source: LCC, adapted from Wachtel and McCold (2000).

Key point

The ideas of restorative services link very well with a family support orientation that emphasises the place of *purposeful support*. Here clear boundaries and parameters are set out alongside a high level of support and help.

The concepts of restorative practice are gaining currency, with examples of local authorities incorporating it into their children and families and adult care provision. An example of implementation is Gloucestershire local authority: here the principles of empowering and working *with* families frame the whole approach and services are linked

to this. More details are available at: http://www.gloucestershire.
gov.uk/health-and-social-care/children-young-people-and-families/
restorative-practice-in-gloucestershire/.

Based on the principles of the better known restorative justice ideas,
which suggested different and more personalised ways to repair harm and
move forward, these are widely applied in the justice and youth justice
fields. The use of restorative models has been shown to help communities, groups and organisations to reduce crime, violence or bullying and
generally improve relationships. The method is used in many schools
and educational settings, especially to resolve issues such as discipline
and bullying (Costello et al., 2010). One particular benefit is that social
capital of individuals and groups can be strengthened (International Institute for Restorative Practices) through better functioning and improved
trust: increasing trust in relationships is a core element of bonding social
capital. Also at the micro level, people's behaviour can be influenced in a
positive way and leadership or functioning of a group enhanced.

The techniques of restorative working are implemented with groups,
which could be a group of family members. Generally, the group gath-
ers in a circle, which helps to promote a sense of community and
togetherness and encourages everybody to take shared responsibility for
the functioning of the circle. Using agreed guidelines the group often
use a 'talking piece' to take turns and listen to each other; circles can
be managed or facilitated by a leader if required and there is a sense
of equality as quieter members also have a say. The language used is
important, with statements made that express the feelings and experience from each person's viewpoint. To help personalise issues, participants in restorative circles are encouraged to use 'I' messages and to
express their needs, with others providing affirmative statements. More
positive words are encouraged from participants, for example, using the
word 'and' rather than 'but', where the latter would suggest an obsta-
cle to resolving an issue. Finally, restorative questions that focus on a
way forward and what needs to happen in the future are focussed on.
There are some variations of the circle method, with more complex
arrangements that are particularly helpful for larger group work. A good
overview can be found at: www.healthiersf.org/RestorativePractices/
Resources, pp. 21–23.

Strengths based and solution focussed

Strengths-based perspectives have gained credibility in recent years,
with their use across family services in the UK and beyond (Malin et
al., 2014). Also in the adult field, person-centred and strengths-based

ideas are evident across a range of services. Strengths based as a particular way of working in the social work field is credited mainly to the work of Dennis Saleeby (1992, 2006); it was based both on a set of ideas and a practical application. Many saw it as representing a real change in terms of refocusing on service users' strengths rather than on risks and deficits. Key components are promoting resilience and coping for service users and the role of social support as a protective factor; underpinned by ecological theory that sees the person in the context of their wider environment. The strengths-based model links well with the new discourse of partnership with service users that has emerged in recent decades where the service user is seen as the expert and there is an emphasis on sharing power with the user and on relationship working.

Roose et al. (2014) have recently suggested that there is a 'family' of strengths-based approaches that have developed in different settings, based on the core values, and that there may be a fragmented implementation. One example is in the adult social care sector: Whittaker et al. (2014) describe a 'surface level' focus on strengths by workers dealing with immediate problems and suggest that a more in-depth application is needed, especially in the context of reductions in provision and quality input and time with individuals. Critiques do suggest that in focussing on building individual-level strengths, it can become closely linked with neoliberal goals of individualism (Gray, 2011). Because of this, Roose et al. (2014) argue that the strengths perspective needs a more political element, considering work in the broader context of poverty and structural inequality. It can therefore be of immense value if wider factors that frame the lives of so many service users are taken into account sufficiently.

Key point

Looking at strengths has frequently been seen as a 'softer' option in child welfare services, particularly when dealing with risk. Also, some argue that strengths-based working becomes eroded in the face of the reality of child protection and that workers struggle to balance the use of their power and authority with empowerment (Roose et al., 2014; Oliver and Charles, 2015). However, utilising a strengths-based perspective in child protection and welfare services has really become an aim for many workers despite the risk averse and managerialist culture that dominate in services (Keddell, 2014).

Solution focussed working is closely linked to a strengths-based orientation. The practitioner taking this angle will focus on finding out what a person's wishes or 'preferred future' is and crucially the steps that may need to be taken to get there. There is an emphasis on language, with the practitioner asking useful questions: in the case of what the person would like to happen in the future, the 'miracle question' is often used – if you could wake up and the problem was completely solved, what would that look like? However there is also a steer towards more concrete and observable steps so that a person's progress towards goals can be readily seen by themselves and by others. Actions are important in the process with the aim of understanding what steps have already been taken and what now needs to be done to achieve the goals. Scaling or measuring progress is seen as an important part of this process, with progress viewed as a driver for further change (Pichot and Dolan, 2014).

Rather than a practitioner giving advice, a change of emphasis is required that invites listening and exploring new possibilities with a service user. The practitioner particularly tries to elicit any 'exceptions' where things have been different or have worked well. Such instances can be reflected on and used to draw on for future actions, providing a sense of hope that goals can be achieved: a useful set of assumptions to guide practice is provided by Myers (2007 in Milner et al., 2015). Additionally, a comprehensive overview of solution focussed models and further detail on their application is provided by Shennan's text (2014), where he suggests the approach is one where '…one person helps another to come up with thoughts, ideas and answers that turn out to be useful for them' (p. 3).

Practice focus

Returning to the example earlier in the chapter, what useful questions would you ask Martina using this solution focussed idea? What specific steps do you think would show her that she was making progress towards her goals for the family?

Signs of Safety

The strengths-based perspective has developed with a strong association to the principles of solution focussed (Oliver and Charles, 2015), which is seen as one of its main areas of practice application, particularly in the 'Signs of Safety' approach. As a specific mode of intervention the Signs of Safety (SoS) initiative originated in Australia

(Turnell and Edwards, 1999). It was developed there in response to the overwhelmingly negative experience of parents and young people in child protection services and a call for greater partnership working. The model has been established by children's services in a number of areas in the UK and is being implemented in different forms internationally. In the UK, up until recently, around 35 English Local Authorities are known to be using a form of SoS in child protection work and child protection conferences (Wheeler and Hogg, 2012). Eileen Munro, Andrew Turnell and Terry Murphy have established a consultancy, with government input, to promote and oversee the implementation and ongoing training around SoS, which is trademarked (see http://munroturnellmurphy.com/). It is based on a new attitude to the sharing of information and decision making that seeks to take a more family-centred view.

Traditional child protection conferences were found to be effective in terms of professionals sharing information around risk but have tended to be *problem centred* rather than *solution focussed*. Parents had described traditional child protection conferences as intimidating and stressful, feeling powerless to have an impact on decisions or to be actively involved. Signs of Safety is essentially a strengths-based model of child protection that utilises solution focussed methods. Professionals in child protection meetings tended to focus on parents' weaknesses whilst not emphasising their strengths and positive qualities (Appleton et al., 2014). Positive relationships between professionals and families are thought to be crucial to achieving outcomes (Bunn, 2013). The specific tools to capture children's and young people's views, such as 'The Three Houses', have been developed and are widely used and are available on the Signs of Safety official website (https://www.signsofsafety.net/).

Some features of SoS are:

➤ Strengths of the family are harnessed to ensure the safety of the child.

➤ Protective factors and strengths of the family are balanced with the level of danger and risk of harm, with a clear focus on the safety of the child.

➤ Use of the assessment resources shifts from the practitioner towards a transparent process that engages with the family.

➤ It helps to build supportive relationships and provides a sense of hope for families as they try to establish change.

➤ The environment is transparent.

➤ The Three Houses and other tools to gain the views of children are incorporated into the process.

Key point

The Signs of Safety initiative seeks to empower families and involve them in partnership to assess and plan a way forward that ensures the protection of the children involved. Whilst working in partnership and involving the family more, the process still holds to a particular child-centred orientation that aims to deliver a robust risk assessment. It appears to hold the promise of helping '...agencies and practitioners' revision of risk assessment as a rigorous, participatory and more hopeful process and practice....' (Turnell et al., 2017: 132).

Practice focus

In a high risk child protection case where the family has two young children, a substantial history of domestic violence, poor parenting capacity and little wider support, the different emphases of the approaches at a child protection conference are shown below. The aim of the child protection conference in both cases will be to make decisions about risk to the children and draw up a plan.

Traditional approach	Signs of Safety approach
■ Risk assessment	■ Quality engagement with the family seen as the key to risk assessment
■ Put supports in place	■ Focus on identifying and drawing on strengths/supports
■ Focus on what life is like for the children	■ Increase resources/quality of life for the children
■ Multi-agency input	■ More emphasis on shared multi-agency solutions

Messages from research

The 'Graded Care Profile' was developed by Dr Srivastava as a risk assessment tool to look at the care parents provided for their child(ren) and help to identify neglect. The tool is used in a number of local authorities in all countries of the UK, and the focus is on early intervention with families and an emphasis on solutions in terms of what needs to change.

▶

◄

Its aims in terms of working with families are to identify parental strengths through a participatory and engaging process and to help parents to better understand the concerns. The tool is interesting in its emphasis on an objective description of parental care across a number of domains, with practitioners finding this particularly useful, as neglect is difficult to assess and measure in practice.

Results from an initial evaluation by Johnson and Cotmore (2015) reported that practitioners found the tool useful in acting as a springboard for change; that it increased understanding of what was happening for a child and what could change. A second evaluation took place after the GCP2 developed following some improvements to the original (Johnson et al., 2015).

Direct work in complex systems

The need for direct work and contact to hear the voice of the child has been highlighted historically by high profile cases, but also repeatedly and more recently in the light of perceived failings in Lord Laming's two reports (2003, 2009) and Eileen Munro's review (2011). Throughout child protection, there is a history of children's voices not being heard: famously in the tragedy of Maria Colwell back in 1974, there was found to be a lack of social work visits, a failure to engage Maria who was not seen alone and an overall focus on the parents' perspectives (Reder and Duncan, 2004). Despite subsequent policy advocating child-centred working, similar cases have persisted where a focus on parents has taken precedence: these cases serve as a reminder to practitioners of the need to actively focus on engaging with the child or young person (Winter, 2011).

Meaningful contact with children and young people by practitioners is felt to still be lacking despite the continued emphasis on this in policy and legislation. The result of investment in bureaucratic systems by social workers and other practitioners at the expense of less direct work with children and families has been highlighted (Broadhurst et al., 2010).

One of the main arguments to increase the level of direct work and contact time with children and young people is simply from a rights basis – children's right to a voice, to be heard and involved. This can be viewed from a general human rights lens and is enshrined in the UN Convention on the Rights of the Child (UNCRC). Both social workers and other practitioners generally want to undertake more direct work to ensure more robust safeguarding along with this clear child-centred perspective.

Across the spectrum of child welfare, of particular importance is the work with more complex cases. Here, factors such as the child's vulnerability, dealing with loss and trauma, and the nature and duration of abuse they have suffered are important. Davies and Lebloch (2013), for example, detail the trust and authenticity required to work effectively with an adolescent in a case of child sexual exploitation. Crucial areas that direct work can focus on are hearing a child's experiences and understanding their wishes and hopes around education, health and their living arrangements. For the particular group of children in care, attachments and relationships are vital, along with issues of loss and trauma recovery. Children who are or have been in care or are involved in the child protection system are often prone to increased vulnerabilities around issues of poor educational attainment, emotional and behavioural difficulties and a number of other risk factors. If children feel they will be heard and taken seriously, they will be less vulnerable to safeguarding issues (Cairns and Brannen, 2005). From a children's rights point of view, there are further benefits from engaging with children as it enables then to develop a more positive sense of identity and self-esteem. Children can become more confident when adults actively listen to their views and develop skills for the future as they become more independent.

Messages from research

O'Reilly and Dolan (2016) carried out a study in relation to social workers undertaking direct work with children. The focus of the research was on age appropriate participation in child welfare assessments in Ireland, taking a child rights perspective. The authors noted that in terms of context, the Irish child welfare system bears the hallmarks of the bureaucratic systems that prevail elsewhere.

The use of play skills training was introduced to enhance social workers' communication with children, with the results pointing to an increased confidence and level of engagement of practitioners with children and young people. It was felt that the skills put into practice ensured more child centredness: they were reportedly better able to focus on the child and the child's voice was heard to a greater and more detailed extent.

Interestingly, workers reported that after including this direct play work, the assessment process also felt safer and the workers felt that they enjoyed their job more, suggesting multiple benefits from this increase in skilled direct contact.

> **Practice focus**
>
> The Communi-CRATE Worksheets are a set of tools that have been devised by the Children's Involvement Team, at Sheffield Local Authority in the UK. The aim of the tools is to assist social workers and practitioners to carry out direct work with children and young people. The worksheets are based around eliciting children's wishes and feelings. A variety of age appropriate sheets enable feelings to be explored as well as experiences and their wishes for the future.
>
> A sample of the worksheets is available at the following link: http://www.sheffkids.co.uk/adultssite/pages/communicrateworksheets.html.

Domestic abuse and violence

A number of approaches to intimate partner violence and abuse have been developing, such as whole population or preventative inputs. Given the increased focus on this issue for young people, these initiatives particularly aimed at school settings are timely. An evaluation by Stanley et al. (2015) as part of the Preventing Domestic Abuse for Children (PEACH) initiative looked at the effectiveness of general population preventative programmes around domestic abuse. There was some evidence found of the effectiveness of such programmes delivered in schools, particularly around changing norms and attitudes amongst pupils. Particular factors appeared to influence the effectiveness of the initiatives and it was suggested that a certain number of children and young people, due to their background and experiences, may need a higher level of input around these issues within the school setting.

At the tertiary end of the spectrum where domestic violence and abuse have occurred within families, some whole family services are developing.

Stanley and Humphreys (2017) analyse the application of whole family provisions to work with domestic violence and abuse. They outline that a number of emergent practices in the area do aim to work with the whole family and that this follows general trends in family support and holistic family initiatives. The development of these are welcomed by many and seen as an antidote to the routine response of social care agencies, with a focus on engaging all family members and building partnerships with the family. However, caution is required with the models: perpetrators are typically seen separately, and rigorous and sensitive risk assessment is required to avoid some of the complexities of working with perpetrators concurrently.

Leeds City Council, as part of their overall focus on restorative and early intervention services with families, 'Family Valued', has begun the use of family group conferences (FGCs) in cases of domestic abuse, as part of a wider revised, multi-agency approach. Early indications of this use of the service have shown that with careful risk management, support for the victim and a focus on safety, conferences can produce helpful outcomes and the abuse is less hidden. The recent evaluation of the service (Mason et al., 2017) found that three approaches were taken to FGCs, with many able to utilise wider maternal family support, some resolving issues with the involvement of perpetrators and some involving perpetrators on a restorative basis. FGCs have been referred to earlier in this text, but here we can see the way they can potentially be developed for particular issues. By their nature, FGCs really address critical issues in partnership and participation with families. Having become a central tool in some countries such as New Zealand where their use is now enshrined in legislation, elsewhere their popularity is growing and the idea is seen as innovative. Previous research had shown that the conferences could be successfully held in situations where there has been substantial abuse, such as domestic violence (Pennell and Burford, 2000). However other studies are less clear on the longer term impact of FGCs on child protection issues, for example the longitudinal follow-up Swedish study on re-referrals to child protection (Sundell and Vinnerljung, 2004). The substantial and innovative use of FGCs in this local authority context may provide useful insight for the child protection field when longer term outcomes emerge.

International example: The ideas of social pedagogy

The concepts of social pedagogy are commonly thought to involve a 'heart and head' orientation, where well-being is promoted through both social and educational working. The model is utilised in many European countries and there is an increasing interest developing in the UK. Social pedagogy can be seen as both an academic discipline and a practice method that underpins work with children and youth.

Janer and Ucar (2017) summarise that it originated as a response to dealing with risk and vulnerability for young people. Its more limited application in the UK has initially taken a narrower focus on children's residential care. Hatton (2013) advocates the

▶

◀

potential of its wider use in social work and in the children and families field generally. He suggests that the key features are:

- Relationship building, partnerships and inclusion as important factors, particularly those based on equality, partnership and inclusion;

- Promoting risk-taking to develop the child or young person; and

- A holistic approach to the person as a whole, and the different levels of their environment, including the wider social and economic environment.

It is linked to building resilience by helping young people encounter and cope with challenges in a way they can learn from (Joslyn, 2015).

Further information can be sought at the following website: http://www.socialpedago-gyuk.com/.

Largely used in residential care in European countries, the practical skills of workers are valued, with domestic and routine activities seen as an opportunity to share and learn (Hatton, 2013). This has clear links to a family support approach, with a focus on a holistic outlook but also equality and empowering young people through a range of practical, social and emotional supports.

Changing behaviours and solving problems

Family drug and alcohol courts (FDACs) are a new initiative that aims to assist with problem solving for complex family situations in the family court in relation to care proceedings in child protection. Its aims are to tackle what have become known as the trilogy of factors in such cases (Brandon, 2008), namely substance misuse, mental health and domestic violence and abuse. The initiative was set up originally by judge Creighton in the London area, and has since been rolled out to 15 local authorities, receiving funding from the DfE Children's Social Care Innovation Programme. After referral to the service and an assessment, families are allocated a key worker who carries out direct work with the parents, along with multi-agency coordination of relevant services.The fact that each case is dealt with by the same judge at review and there is specialist staff support leads to a therapeutic element combined with the monitoring of the family (Sawyer and Burton, 2016).

The initiative is seen as being a successful approach. Motivating parents to work towards outcomes is central to the technique, which is therapeutic and also reviews progress robustly through a 'trial for change' period. An evaluation of the service showed that there were higher rates of reduced substance misuse, greater prospects of family reunification and family stability. More information on the evaluation and some of the early outcomes can be found at their website: http://fdac.org.uk/.

Although not a new method, the value of motivational interviewing as a technique and a theoretical basis in relation to changing behaviour has been renewed. This model is seen as being most effective with very challenging service users or those resistant to change. It draws on counseling skills and a person-centred vision, utilizing empathy as a tool to understand the person's ambivalence to change. Skills utilized by the practitioner include reflective listening to understand the person's point of view and deal with resistance to change. Along with listening, the other important element is a verbally based process that relies on the worker to draw out information during an interaction and to convey this information back to the person, working on the gap between a person's values (or how they would like to be) and their actual behavior.

The cycle of change on which the technique is based was outlined by Prochaska et al. (1992) and is a widely used application. The stages include the pre-contemplation stage, where the problem perceived by the practitioner is not yet acknowledged or recognized by the service user. This moves on to where a person is contemplating the possibility of change, followed by stages where the person is preparing to change, then takes action to change and finally works to maintain the change. A particularly useful aspect of using this conceptual cycle is for the practitioner to better understand the responses, which will be very different depending on where the person is on the 'cycle'. Although originating and widely used in the substance misuse field, the cycle is applicable to any area of required change and resistance; Miller and Rollnick's (2012) text is a useful practitioner guide to the techniques.

Messages from research

Benefits of motivational interviewing are that it is seen to build a person's self-efficacy in terms of a belief they can change and seeks to avoid impasse or counterproductive arguments (Payne, 2014).

Forrester et al. (2008) analyzed a series of simulated interviews by social workers; their findings showed that the workers were poor at displaying empathy to the service user role players and that they often adopted a confrontational style which seemed to foster further resistance from service users. In a later paper, Forrester et al. (2012) explored the value of utilizing motivational interviewing skills in child protection social work: crucially, in this area of work, parents are likely to be resistant to change.

▶

◄

The authors discuss studies that highlight the importance of listening and honest communication with parents. The roots of resistance to change are complex and varied, but the application of motivational interviewing skills is the focus it provides on the quality of interaction with the service user.

Further reading

Bunn, A., 2013. Signs of Safety in England: An NSPCC commissioned report on the signs of safety model in child protection.
This report from the NSPCC is available from their website and provides a detailed outline of key findings about the model.

International Institute for Restorative Practices. Available at: https://www.iirp. edu/.
This website provides a range of information and evaluation in relation to restorative practices and their application.

Johnson, R., Smith, E. & Fisher, H., 2015. *Testing the Reliability and Validity of the Graded Care Profile Version 2 (GCP2)*. London: NSPCC.
An outline of the approach that has been adapted by a number of local authorities.

O'Reilly, L. & Dolan, P., 2016. The voice of the child in social work assessments: Age-appropriate communication with children. *The British Journal of Social Work, 46*(5), pp. 1191–1207.
A journal article that highlights possibilities for meaningful engagement of social workers with children.

9

Conclusion – Current Themes and the Future for Family Support Approaches

This concluding chapter is an opportunity to draw together some of the dominant current themes in the family support arena. Many of the issues discussed in previous chapters will be summarised in the current policy and practice context. A reflection on the future prospects for the continued development of family support as an emerging discipline and an area of working, and the possibilities and challenges of future directions, is presented.

➢ Prevention and the early intervention agenda

➢ Family poverty and inequality

➢ Relationship-based practice and the place of social work

➢ The para-professional and the role of the private/voluntary/independent (PVI) sector

➢ Looking to the future: Family support in a globalised context

Prevention and the early intervention agenda

Previous chapters have outlined some policy approaches that have gained currency in recent decades around prevention, early intervention and the preferred term 'early help' (Frost et al., 2015). In the recent context of austerity and the rollback of many services, the language and policy shift is still clearly towards prevention with remedial services seen as far more costly. The ideas of the costs and benefits of such early help provision has been very much linked to the evidence-informed practice movement, the focus on outcomes and value for money.

Early intervention itself, broadly defined as 'early in the problem', has to an extent been replaced with a focus primarily on the early years. This could be seen in the 'Supporting Families' document from New Labour in the UK which was a turning point in family policy, drawn from the 'first three years' in the US, with its focus on early childhood (Macvarish et al., 2015). The needs of children under 5 years old have taken on somewhat of a global significance, with groups like the World Health Organisation and World Bank viewing services for early childhood as being a key time to invest to equalise opportunity and develop human capital in the upcoming generation (Morabito et al., 2013). This focus has been based on findings from neuroscience about young children's development, but there are critiques of how it is applied, with the emphasis on future results rather than the child in the present (Lister, 2006). The Allen Review (2011) in particular was criticised for the emphasis on the 'emotional wiring' of the child, rather than their holistic development (Wastell and White, 2017). The pioneering work of Rutter amongst others has highlighted both risk and vulnerability in early childhood but also the plasticity of the human brain in developing at later stages and in overcoming adverse experiences, along with the crucial role that resilience plays.

From a broader family support perspective it is important to acknowledge that early childhood is indeed an important time to invest in services, with the evidence showing the benefits of doing so, and the child rights to provision at a time in their development that may benefit them most. Therefore there are good reasons to focus on early years but not to the exclusion of input throughout childhood or where at different points, due to life circumstances, problems occur. Different needs can occur across the life course and the broader perspective is important so that services for older children and adolescents are not overlooked. From a support perspective, the ideas of neuroscience can be carefully used to argue for more preventative services (Connolly, 2017), preferably across the age ranges.

Key point

A family support orientation emphasises both early years intervention and an 'early in the problem' view across the life course. This latter emphasis seeks to ensure that a broad perspective in relation to provision across the lifespan is maintained. As we know that family policy is always based on views and constructions of families (Foley, 2011), this wider lens is important.

A spin-off from the focus on young children through early years' intervention has been an increased lens on parenting (Holt, 2011). Parenting advice has now become quite commercialised (Daly, 2013): an example is the growing number of prescribed parenting courses, some of which originate from the US, and the increase in popular television programmes and online videos on parenting techniques. As the family and children have become focus points, there is a move to placing expectations of overcoming child deprivation and poverty, particularly on mothers (Edwards et al., 2015). This runs alongside other developments in the conceptualisation of family overall as a key area where governments can invest and intervene, along with increased surveillance, especially of poor families. Certainly, within this agenda, a number of excellent and supportive services have emerged as at their core, many parenting and programmes are located in the principles of partnership and empowerment with families. Along with the benefits, however, there can be pressure on parents. It is important for family support to be cognizant of the wider social contexts when considering the benefits and drawbacks of different services.

> **Key point**
>
> A tension between supporting vulnerable families and child protection functions is central in the child welfare field in contemporary Western systems. Kirton (2008) depicts this as a tension between a child rescue (protection) and a family support approach, which he argues is still not well resolved. Governments are more interested in intervening in families as outlined above, but not always with a supportive aim. As child protection continues to focus on investigation and risk management, early intervention services themselves can become pulled into this framework (Bilson et al., 2017).

Family poverty and inequality

Policy and views about poverty have moved to put more emphasis on individual responsibility rather than the structural causes of poverty and deprivation. Ideas of 'new poverty management' or increased regulation of the poor through sanctions and conditions have become commonplace in many countries. One example of this is the growth of 'welfare conditionality' in relation to the various restrictions and criteria on benefits payments (see Taylor-Gooby, 2008; Dwyer and Wright, 2014). Thinking in the area of poverty reduction is now largely reduced to employment activation measures, simply getting adults into paid employment. There has been a general shift in government attitudes to inequality, with moral overtones, placing explanations for the causes of poverty with individual and behaviours (Smethurst, 2017). This is mirrored in public perceptions where the prevalence and causes are less widely appreciated, although research from the Joseph Rowntree Foundation suggests some shift towards a more understanding attitude in the light of precarious employment (Hall et al., 2014). In-work poverty has been growing, with concerns from leading charity The Trussel Trust that use of foodbanks may become the norm (Butler, 2016).

Within this overall context, however, reducing child poverty is still an important goal globally. Although progress in reducing child poverty was made in England under the former Labour government and the enactment of the Child Poverty Act 2010, this has stagnated with the change in law and policy. In Wales, reports showing a lack of progress in tackling poverty led to a strategic approach with the 'Flying Start' programme for families with young children living in disadvantaged areas as part of the Tackling Poverty agenda. The Child Poverty Action Group (CPAG) is a leading organisation campaigning around child poverty, and Barnardo's campaigns in all five nations, including Ireland. Recent figures suggest that in the UK the number of children in relative poverty will have risen from 2.3 to 3.6 million by 2020 (CPAG). In the wider context, poor families are disproportionately represented in lower outcomes across the board. Some of the effects are poor health, stress, stigma, mental ill-health and reduced parenting capacity. There is an increasing recognition also of the micro effects on children's lives, with research showing the reduced opportunities to participate in activities and social events with their peers (Ridge, 2004). In the practice field, however, commentators have noted the lack of attention given by social workers to issues of poverty and deprivation in assessments (Jack and Donnellan, 2013). For a family support approach, as part of the social care spectrum, it is vital that issues of poverty, inequality and inclusion that form the backdrop to so many families' lives are fully considered. Poverty and inequality are likely to increase and impact on the effectiveness of services for individual families in this context.

Messages from research

A spotlight on poverty

A study has recently been published by Bywaters and colleagues: *The relationship between poverty, child abuse and neglect: an evidence review* (2016). This was commissioned by the Joseph Rowntree Foundation and reviewed literature in order to

▶

◄

analyse links between poverty and child protection. The report outlined the strong association between families' socio-economic status and children's chances of being subject to abuse or neglect and makes suggestions for anti-poverty policies to consider this. The complex relationships of factors around poverty are discussed with health, environmental factors, stress, mental health and housing interlinked.

In a further two-year study funded by the Nuffield Foundation, Bywaters et al. explored the links between inequality and children's services in the *Child Welfare Inequalities Project*. The study examines quantitative data and the team have produced a number of related articles on the relationship between poverty, inequality and child abuse and neglect, considering if children's services reflect, reinforce or reduce these social inequalities.

A link to this project and further details can be found at: http://www.coventry.ac.uk/ research/research-directories/current-projects/2014/child-welfare-inequality-uk/.

Relationship-based practice and the place of social work

Relationship-based approaches are seen as an important pillar of practice (Ruch et al., 2010) and there are renewed arguments about their centrality and the need to return to such a focus, as opposed to what has become the bureaucratic focus of current services. Morris (2013) for example found that in terms of assessment, 'fleeting visits' by workers meant that they didn't see the full picture of what was happening in a family. Jones et al. (2015: 157) suggest a '…reclaiming of the space for psychosocial relationship based practice'. Many service developments that have been discussed through the book are seen as strengthening relationships with and between multi-professional teams and families. Relationship building with service users requires a positive therapeutic alliance and a collaborative partnership. In emphasizing the role of relationships we are reflecting the voice of service users: research shows us the value that individuals and families place on relationships (Spratt and Callan, 2004).

In services dominated by bureaucracy, time spent in relationship building is an important issue: certainly many workers bemoan the lack of contact time with families afforded to their work, but it can be suggested that, with the right approach: 'Even a brief encounter with a child and family can have therapeutic value and pave the way for ongoing relationship-based practice' (Teater, 2014: 18). This suggests that limited time in itself need not be a complete barrier. The research cited in

Chapter 8 further indicates that time spent differently where a range of skills are employed with children and young people can ensure a deeper level of engagement. From a family support perspective, the benefits that develop from relationship building are crucial both to the intervention and the development of networks for service users, drawing on the tenets of emotional and esteem support that provide a valuable resource to service users.

Key point

The key worker role really draws on the use of relationship-based models. The key worker crucially brings together the emotional and practical support that is so valued by service users (McKeown, 2013).

In terms of the place of social work, a number of innovative and emerging practices have been discussed throughout the book. For the social work profession, however, it can be challenging to consider how some of these models can be applied at the child protection end of the spectrum. Ideas such as restorative working or family group conferences can be more easily applied to less complex cases, whereas higher risk cases fit less well. The direction of social work in England and other jurisdictions really emphasises the child protection arena, with the wider welfare context less of a focus and increasingly seen as the role of other agencies (Parton, 2014). In a worldwide context, there are strong links between social work and wider community work whereas, in Western societies, social work with families has largely operated on an individualist model (Parton, 2005). Holman (1988) provides a useful outline of the history of social work in the UK where its roots were formerly in broader community and locality based settings. The recently narrower remit, with wider welfare seen as more peripheral to social work, has challenged the values and inclusive perspective of the profession with its technical, managerial focus (Rogowski, 2011; Jordan and Drakeford, 2012).

The principles of family support, however, could usefully be seen as an opportunity for social workers in this context, in particular, up-skilling practitioners around some of the components of direct work (see Dolan and O'Reilly, 2016) or in relationship-building skills (see Forrester et al., 2008). The Signs of Safety model outlined in the previous chapter offers not only an empowering approach that is much valued by families, but also a skilled and thorough risk assessment. There may also be a valued role for social work in activating social networks for families (Sheppard, 2007). The Children's Social Care Innovation program in England and the move towards recognition of new practices elsewhere potentially can provide a valuable impetus for social work to develop in these areas. At its roots, there are very close links and a complementary synergy between social work and family support (Mc Cormack, 2012).

The para-professional and the role of the PVI sector

The majority of work both in the social care sector and the child and family sector is undertaken by paraprofessional staff with varying levels of qualification. The professionalization of the social care sector has been a policy aim over recent years. The setting up of the former CWDC in the UK was an important step in this regard, in developing frameworks and standards for the children's workforce. Since then Skills for Care has provided this for both the adult and child fields, along with advice for the sector around their implementation. As part of 'Skills for Care and Development', Skills for Care has partner organisations in the three UK nations. There have been various initiatives to encourage the development of accredited qualifications across the sector. The proposed new apprenticeships and higher apprenticeships in England are a welcome step forward and are aimed at those working and managing others in both community-based and other settings. These developments suggest the potential of a more flexible and integrative process for the workforce, which is a key feature of work-based learning (Helyer, 2015).

This wider view of the sector is important, given the role played by a variety of workers and volunteers and the informal help provided by family and others. Often, it is the relationship building and help provided that contributes to outcomes rather than whether it is provided by a professional or not (Barlow, 2006; Dunst, 2008). With the stronger emphasis on multidisciplinary working and a range of agencies taking responsibility for child and family welfare, this area of work is increasingly complex. Frost et al. (2015) have advocated for the development of the family support workforce, as it is often overshadowed by its near neighbour social work with a higher professional status. It is likely that support roles will continue to be important in terms of direct working and contact with service users, which is often of a more in-depth nature than the professionals, due to the time and other constraints.

Key point

Although many in the social and family care sector may be less qualified and on lower pay scales, much of the work carried out is both crucial and of a high quality, with dedication and flexibility in the settings. The level of skill and ability to engage with families is often exemplary and indeed could provide learning for professional counterparts (Dolan et al., 2007).

The private, voluntary and independent sector has grown to play an increasing part in the spectrum of services as outsourcing and a mixed market of care has expanded in many countries. There are numerous benefits from smaller community-based projects that can be empowering and sometimes service-user led despite being part of the growing marketisation of services (Kenny et al., 2015). Smaller and independent organisations may be able to take on more of a campaigning and advocacy role, having fewer constraints. However there are a number of issues with the bidding and tenders process in an increasingly competitive sector (Whitfield, 2015). In this climate the focus is on measurable outcomes rather than some of the 'softer outcomes', for example, an increase in self-efficacy, which may be harder to evidence, but none the less is valuable for service users. There are issues also with less secure, shorter term funding which can impact on the recruitment and retention of staff. Many social care settings are described by Baines et al. (2014) as being 'lean' in terms of funding, staffing and resources. Often services and individual workers adopt a good deal of agency when operating within such constraints: workers are resourceful and have flexible and creative responses. The examples of holistic support that meet the psychosocial and emotional as well as practical needs of service users that are highlighted in evaluations seem far removed from the realities of restraints of services and budgetary reductions.

Practice focus

The Family Rights group

This charity began as a small organisation; it provides advice, information and help for families who are involved with children's social care. A number of services are also provided, along with advocacy for family members. Its position as an independent

▶

◀

organisation has enabled the group to act as a voice in advocating for carers rights and for more family-orientated services in the child welfare system. This has been an important position as children's services have become more narrowly focussed on risk and many service users feel unfairly treated in the 'system'.

There is a particular focus on family group conferences as a more inclusive and empowering approach, and on enabling families to undertake kinship care. There are links to research studies and useful publications provided that are relevant to those interested in this area of provision. The website with further information is available at: http://www.frg.org.uk.

Looking to the future: Family support in a globalised context

There are some opportunities afforded to the family support discipline in terms of sharing and comparing programmes and initiatives, with the global comparative report in Chapter 1 providing a useful example of this.

However, the rise of neoliberal economies has created challenges for welfare and service advocates. The features of neoliberalism are well documented: with greater globalisation and increased population movement, the emphasis has been on creating a priority for economy/ markets, less state activity, deregulation, and a lower value placed on social policies (Payne, 2014). The dominance of these neoliberal concepts with their key characteristics of a reduced role for the state but increased targeting of resources is problematic for those advocating a firmer and wider embedding of family support. Further still, Garrett (2014) points out that the role of the state is in fact 'reshaped' rather than just reduced. Family support in these circumstances can become 'subsumed' in early intervention/prevention (Frost et al., 2015). Many note that it is the poorest families who are particularly under scrutiny, as an increase in state monitoring is targeted towards particular families seen as 'troubled' (Featherstone et al., 2014). Notably, non-stigmatising support such as universal provision is being reduced (Bilson et al., 2017). Family support arguably needs to take an anti-neoliberal stance in relation to a system where inequality is increased and risk takes precedence over need.

Gilbert (2012: 535) suggests that a number of countries are converging in terms of their approach to '…moderate versions of the child protection and family service orientations incorporated within the more comprehensive approach of child development…', but that this development is uncertain in the current financial restraints. Family support and preventative services can be subject to cutbacks if they are seen as an 'add on' rather than a central core of provision that is rooted in a clear rationale. Exploring the UK experience from the New Labour government through to the present, Canavan et al. (2016) caution that family support services can be in a precarious position in policy terms. Interestingly, their analysis suggests that family support is usefully seen in the overall welfare context of a country. In the UK example, the overall residual approach to services was the backdrop against which the government attempted to layer widely available developmental services, such as Sure Start and youth services, as part of their 'progressive universalism' (Sheppard, 2012). With the squeeze on public resources that followed, and a change in government, these services have proved vulnerable to both ideological and budgetary restraints, with funding now reduced (Jack and Donnellan, 2013). As Whipple and Whyte (2009) point out, it is harder to 'prove' that prevention works or is cost effective, which matters in times of budgetary restraints.

A recent report from Action for Children (2013) has highlighted the importance of early intervention, prevention and support work. However, the report also highlights the reduced funding to supportive services in the UK that has been characteristic of countries focussed on implementing austerity cutbacks. Taking an overview of wider services including youth services and schools funding, the picture is similar (Action for children, 2013; NYA, 2014), with a press release from Barnardo's (2015) highlighting that children's centre funding has been cut by almost one-half since 2010 and calling for these early intervention and family support services to be prioritised. Multiple sources of research and evidence point to the benefits and indeed cost benefits of support services; however, budgets at the frontline do not reflect this. In adult social care similarly, resources are closely tied with health services and the looming 'crisis of care' funding. Interestingly the recent Labour party manifesto in the UK, and the resurgence of the its electoral appeal based on this, called into question the austerity project and gained much credibility: a move to universal service provision being extended was mooted along with wider ecological factors being addressed such as housing (Courtney, 2017).

Key point

There is a broad consensus around the concepts of prevention and early intervention (Action for Children, 2013; Early Intervention Foundation). However, the complexity of supports in the wider welfare system, the effects of cutbacks due to austerity policy and context of increased inequality is arguably incompatible with this.

The need for family support is possibly greater than ever due to increased pressure on families and rising inequality. There is a hopeful and essential place for the field if it is seen as a policy choice but also as a coherent set of ideas and practices that can be applied in multifaceted ways, by different practitioners in a range of settings. The continuing development of the family support area and its core evidence base can add to the arguments for extending rather than retrenching family supportive services:

> ...based in approaches of empowerment, restorative practice and partnership, we believe that family support plays a crucial role, particularly in times of rapid social, political and economic change which tend to take a heavy toll on families and their children...

(Frost et al., 2015: 9).

Much of the analysis throughout the book has suggested a tentatively positive perspective that very service-user focussed provision can still operate within more restrictive contexts and can help to shift policy and debates. Some of the features of a more developmental provision certainly seem to be gaining ground in the strengths- and relational-based approaches. Munro's UK report was an important step in this regard because it promoted innovation and a refocusing on such issues in children's services (Vincent, 2015). As Canavan et al. (2016: 125) point out, despite the push for evidence-based services framed by neoliberal objectives:

> ...there is also an emerging commitment to an empowering, preventative and rights-based value base.

Further reading

Action for Children, 2013. *Losing in the Long Run*. Available at: https://www. actionforchildren.org.uk/media/5826/losing_in_the_long_run.pdf.
A timely and important report making the case for support and intervention.

Canavan, J., Pinkerton, J. & Dolan, P., 2016. *Understanding Family Support: Policy, Practice and Theory*. Jessica Kingsley Publishers.
This text provides a comprehensive and global analysis of family support in the current context.

Featherstone, B., Morris, K., White, S. & White, S., 2014. *Re-imagining Child Protection: Towards Humane Social Work with Families*. Policy Press.

Covering the child protection and welfare systems, this book sets out key arguments.

Frost, N., Abbott, S. & Race, T., 2015. *Family Support: Prevention, Early Intervention and Early Help*. John Wiley & Sons.

Along with practice applications, this text sets out the all-important policy context for family support.

References

Abrams, L.S. & Moio, J.A., 2009. Critical race theory and the cultural competence dilemma in social work education. *Journal of Social Work Education*, 45(2), pp. 245–261.

Action for Children, 2013. *Losing in the Long Run*. Available at: https://www.actionforchildren.org.uk/media/5826/losing_in_the_long_run.pdf.

Action for Children, *The Dundee Project*, Available at: www.actionforchildren.org.uk.

Adams, R., ed., 2011. *Working with Children and Families: Knowledge and Contexts for Practice*. Palgrave Macmillan.

Adams, R., Dominelli, L. & Payne, M., 2009. *Practising Social Work in a Complex World*. Palgrave Macmillan.

Addis, S., Davies, M., Greene, G., MacBride-Stewart, S. & Shepherd, M., 2009. The health, social care and housing needs of lesbian, gay, bisexual and transgender older people: A review of the literature. *Health & Social Care in the Community*, 17(6), pp. 647–658.

Age UK. Website, Available at: https://www.ageuk.org.uk/.

Alcock, C., Daly, G. & Griggs, E., 2014. *Introducing Social Policy*. Routledge.

Aldgate, J., 2015. The place of attachment theory in social work with children and families. In Lishman, J., ed., *Handbook for Practice Learning in Social Work and Social Care: Knowledge and Theory* (pp. 57–73). Jessica Kingsley Publishers.

Allen, G., 2011. *Early Intervention: The Next Steps*. HM Government *Alzheimers Society*. Website, Available at: https://www.alzheimers.org.uk/info/20079/dementia_friendly_communities.

An Evaluation of the Standing Together project. The Mental Health Foundation. Available at: https://www.mentalhealth.org.uk/publications/evaluation-standing-together-project.

Appleton, J.V., Terletsi, E. & Coombes, L., 2014. Implementing the strengthening families approach to child protection conferences. *British Journal of Social Work*, 45(5), pp. 1395–1414.

Ashton, K., Bellis, M., Davies, H.K. & Hughes, K., 2015. *Welsh Adverse Childhood Experiences (ACE) Study*. Public Health Wales *Attachment and Relationship-Based Practice*. Available at: http://arpractice.org.uk/index.html.

Ba, S., 2017. Families with young children, precarious work and social justice. In Mealey, A.M., Jarvis, P., Doherty, J. & Fook, J., eds., *Everyday Social Justice and Citizenship: Perspectives for the 21st Century*. Routledge.

Baginsky, M., Moriarty, J., Manthorpe, J., Beecham, J. & Hickman, B., 2017. Evaluation of signs of safety in 10 pilots, July 2017. Department for Education.

Bailey, D., 2012. *Interdisciplinary Working in Mental Health*. Palgrave Macmillan.

Baines, D., Charlesworth, S., Turner, D. & O'Neill, L., 2014. Lean social care and worker identity: The role of outcomes, supervision and mission. *Critical Social Policy*, *34*(4), pp. 433–453.

Baldock, J., Mitton, L., Manning, N. & Vickerstaff, S., eds., 2011. *Social Policy*. Oxford University Press.

Barker, J. & Hodes, D., 2007. *The Child in Mind: A Child Protection Handbook* (3rd edn). Routledge.

Barlow, J., 2006. Home visiting for parents of pre-school children in the UK. In McAuley, C., Pecora, P. & Rose, W., eds., *Enhancing the Well-Being of Children and Families through Effective Interventions. International Evidence for Practice* (pp. 46–57). London: Jessica Kingsley.

Barlow, J. & Calam, R., 2011. A public health approach to safeguarding in the 21st century. *Child Abuse Review*, *20*(4), pp. 238–255.

Barnardos. *Government must act to help councils protect vital early years services*. Barnardos, Available at: www.barnardos.org.uk.

Barnardos, 2015. New govt must stop drain in children's centre funding, Press release, available at: http://www.barnardos.org.uk/news/media_centre/New-Govt-must-stop-drain-in-childrens-centre-funding/press_releases.htm?ref=104834

Barnes, J., Ball, M., Meadows, P., McLeish, J. & Belsky, J., 2008. *Nurse-Family Partnership Programme – First Year Pilot Sites in England*. Report to DCSF, May 2008.

Barnes, V., 2015. Skills for inter-professional social work practice. In Davies, K. & Jones, R., eds., *Skills for Social Work Practice*, pp. 178–195. London: Palgrave.

Bartholomew, L., 2015. Child abuse linked to beliefs in witchcraft. *Transnational Social Review*, *5*(2), pp. 193–198.

Bartoli, A., ed., 2013. *Anti-racism in Social Work Practice*. Critical Publishing.

Bécares, L., 2013. *Which Ethnic Groups have the Poorest Health? Ethnic Health Inequalities M 1991 to 2011. Centre on Dynamics of Ethnicity (CoDE) Briefing*. Manchester: Manchester University.

Beddoe, L. 2014. Feral families, troubled families: The spectre of the underclass in New Zealand. *New Zealand Sociology*, *29*(3), p. 51.

Belcher, J.R., Peckuonis, E.V. & Deforge, B.R., 2011. Family capital: Implications for interventions with families. *Journal of Family Social Work*, *14*(1), pp. 68–85.

Bernard, C. & Gupta, A., 2006. Black African children and the child protection system. *British Journal of Social Work*, *38*(3), pp. 476–492.

Bhamra, M.K., 2016. *The Challenges of Justice in Diverse Societies: Constitutionalism and Pluralism*. Routledge.

Bhatti-Sinclair, M.K., 2011. *Anti-racist Practice in Social Work*. Palgrave Macmillan.

Bhatti-Sinclair, K. & Price, D., 2015. Evaluation of serious case reviews and anti-racist practice. In Williams, C. & Graham, M.J., eds., 2015. *Social Work in a Diverse Society: Transformative Practice with Black and Minority Ethnic Individuals and Communities*. Policy Press.

Bhatti-Sinclair, K. & Colin Smethurst, C., 2017. *Diversity, Difference and Dilemmas: Analysing Concepts and Developing Skills.* Open University.

Bhopal, K. & Myers, M., 2009. Gypsy, Roma and Traveller pupils in schools in the UK: Inclusion and 'good practice'. *International Journal of Inclusive Education, 13*(3), pp. 299–314.

Bilson, A., Featherstone, B. & Martin, K., 2017. How child protection's 'investigative turn' impacts on poor and deprived communities. *Family Law Journal, 47*(4), pp. 416–419.

Birmingham Poverty Truth Commission, {online}. Available at: www.brumpovertytruth.org.

Blackburn, C.M., Spencer, N.J. & Read, J.M., 2010. Prevalence of childhood disability and the characteristics and circumstances of disabled children in the UK: Secondary analysis of the family resources survey. *BMC Pediatrics, 10*(1), p. 21.

Bond-Taylor, S., 2015. Dimensions of family empowerment in work with so-called 'troubled' families. *Social Policy and Society, 14*(3), pp. 371–384.

Bonoli, G., George, V. & Taylor-Gooby, P., 2000. *European Welfare Futures.* Polity Press.

Boon, B., & Farnsworth, J., 2011. Social exclusion and poverty: Translating social capital into accessible resources. *Social Policy and Administration, 45*(5), pp. 507–524.

Bourdieu, P., 2011. The forms of capital. *Cultural Theory: An Anthology, 1,* pp. 81–93.

Bowlby, J., 2005. *A Secure Base: Clinical Applications of Attachment Theory* (Vol. 393). Taylor & Francis.

Bowpitt, G., Dwyer, P., Sundin, E. & Weinstein, M., 2013. Places of sanctuary for 'the undeserving'? Homeless people's day centres and the problem of conditionality. *British Journal of Social Work, 44*(5), pp. 1251–1267.

Bracke, P., Christiaens, W. & Verhaeghe, M., 2008. Self-esteem, self-efficacy, and the balance of peer support among persons with chronic mental health problems. *Journal of Applied Social Psychology, 38*(2), pp. 436–459.

Brady, R., 2014. *The Costs of Not Caring: Supporting English Care Leavers into Independence.* Barnardos: Barkinside.

Brandon, M., 2008. Analysing child deaths and serious injury through abuse and neglect: What can we learn?: A biennial analysis of serious case reviews 2003–2005.

Brandon, M., 2009. *Understanding Serious Case Reviews and their Impact: A Biennial Analysis of Serious Case Reviews 2005–07.* London: Department for Education and Skills (DfES).

Bretherington, J. & Pleace, N., 2015. *Housing First in England.* Available at: www.changing-lives.org.uk.

Bright, G., ed., 2015. *Youth Work: Histories, Policy and Contexts.* Palgrave Macmillan.

Bristow, J., 2013. Reporting the riots: Parenting culture and the problem of authority in media analysis of August 2011. *Sociological Research Online, 18*(4) (29 November).

Broadhurst, K., Hall, C., Wastell, D., White, S. & Pithouse, A., 2010. Risk, instrumentalism and the humane project in social work: Identifying the informal logics of risk management in children's statutory services. *British Journal of Social Work, 40*(4), pp. 1046–1064.

Bronfenbrenner, U., 1974. *A Report on Longitudinal Evaluations of Preschool Programs: Is Early Intervention Effective?*. US Department of Health, Education, and Welfare, Office of Human Development, Office of Child Development, Children's Bureau.

Bronfenbrenner, U., 2009. *The Ecology of Human Development*. Harvard University Press.

Brooks, J.E., 2006. Strengthening resilience in children and youths: Maximizing opportunities through the schools. *Children & Schools, 28*(2), pp. 69–76.

Brown, K. & Rutter, L., 2008. *Critical Thinking for Social Work*. SAGE.

Buchanan, E., Poet, H., Sharp, C., Easton, C. & Featherstone, G. 2015. *'Child Neglect is Everyone's Business'. Achieving a Greater Sense of Shared Responsibility for Tackling Neglect: Findings from LARC 6*. Slough: NFER.

Bunn, A. 2013. Signs of safety in England: An NSPCC commissioned report on the signs of safety model in child protection.

Burnham, D., 2016. *The Social Worker Speaks: A History of Social Workers through the Twentieth century*. Routledge.

Butler, P., 2016. *Interview Emma Revie: Why Food Banks Must Never Become the Norm*. The Guardian {online}. Available at: https://www.theguardian.com/society/2018/apr/24/food-banks-norm-trussell-trust-emma-revie.

Bywaters, P., Bunting, L., Davidson, G., Hanratty, J., Mason, W., McCartan, C. & Steils, N., 2016. *The Relationship between Poverty, Child Abuse and Neglect: An Evidence Review*. Available at: http://www.coventry.ac.uk/research/research-directories/current-projects/2014/child-welfare-inequality-uk.

C4EO, 2010. *Grasping the Nettle: Early Intervention for Children, Families and Communities*. London: Centre for Excellence and Outcomes in Children and Young Peoples Services. Available at: http://www.c4eo.org.uk/themes/earlyintervention/files/early_intervention_grasping_the_nettle_full_report.pdf.

C4EO, 2010. *The Views and Experiences of Children and Young People Who Have been through the Child Protection/Safeguarding System*. Available at: http://archive.c4eo.org.uk/themes/safeguarding/default.aspx?themeid=11&accesstypeid=1.

C4EO, 2017. *Devon's Multi Agency Safeguarding Hub (MASH)*. Available at: http://www.c4eo.org.uk/local-practice/emerging-practice-examples/devon%E2%80%99s-multi-agency-safeguarding-hub-(mash).aspx.

Cabinet Office, 2016. *Community Life Survey 2015–16 Statistical Bulletin*.

Čačinovič Vogrinčič, G., 2016. Social work with families: The theory and practice of co-creating processes of support and help. In Mešl, N. & Kodele, T., eds., *Co-creating Processes of Help: Collaboration with Families in the Community*. Ljubljana: Faculty of Social Work.

Cairns, L. & Brannen, M., 2005. Promoting the human rights of children and young people: The 'investing in children' experience. *Adoption & Fostering, 29*(1), pp. 78–87.

Canavan, J., Pinkerton, J. & Dolan, P., 2016. *Understanding Family Support: Policy, Practice and Theory*. Jessica Kingsley Publishers.

Care Act, 2014. London: The Stationery Office.

Carr, D.C. & Gunderson, J.A., 2016. The third age of life: Leveraging the mutual benefits of intergenerational engagement. *Public Policy & Aging Report, 26*(3), pp. 83–87.

Casey, L. 2012. *Listening to Troubled Families. Department for Communities and Local Government*. London: Crown copyright.

Center for Disease Control and Prevention. Website, Available at: https://www.cdc.gov/.

Child Poverty Action Group. Website, Available at: www.cpag.org.uk.

Children Act, 1989. London: The Stationery Office.

Children Act, 2004. London: The Stationery Office.

Children's Workforce Development Council. Website, Available at: http://webarchive.nationalarchives.gov.uk/20120119192332/http://www.cwdcouncil.org.uk/.

Christie, A. & Walsh, T., 2015 Social work in a globalised Ireland. In: Christie, A., Featherstone, B., Quin, S. & Walsh, T., eds., *Social Work in Ireland: Challenges and Continuities*. Basingstoke: Palgrave Macmillan.

Churchill, H., 2011. *Parental Rights and Responsibilities: Analysing Social Policy and Lived Experiences*. Policy Press.

Churchill, H. & Fawcett, B., 2016. Refocusing on early intervention and family support: A review of child welfare reforms in New South Wales, Australia. *Social Policy and Society, 15*(2), pp. 303–316.

Clark, C., 2015. Integration, exclusion and the moral 'othering' of Roma migrant communities in Britain. In Smith, M., ed., *Moral Regulation*, pp. 43–56. Bristol: Policy Press.

Clayton, C.L., 2014. 'With my parents I can tell them anything': Intimacy levels within British Chinese families. *International Journal of Adolescence and Youth, 19*(1), pp. 22–36.

Coleman, J.S., 1988. Social capital in the creation of human capital. *American Journal of Sociology, 94*, pp. S95–S120.

Collins, M., Langer, S., Welch, V., Wells, E., Hatton, C., Robertson, J. & Emerson, E., 2013. A break from caring for a disabled child: Parent perceptions of the uses and benefits of short break provision in England. *British Journal of Social Work, 44*(5), pp. 1180–1196.

Coppock, V. & Dunn, B., 2009. *Understanding Social Work Practice in Mental Health*. Sage.

Connolly, M., 2017. Concluding thoughts: Informal and formal support for vulnerable children and families. In Connolly, M., ed., *Beyond the Risk Paradigm in Child Protection: Current Debates and New Directions*.

Coogan, D., 2011. Child-to-parent violence: Challenging perspectives on family violence. *Child Care in Practice, 17*(4), pp. 347–358.

Corby, B., Shemmings, D. & Wilkins, D., 2012. *Child Abuse: An Evidence Base for Confident Practice*. McGraw-Hill Education.

Cornes, M., Joly, L., O'Halloran, S. & Manthorpe, J., 2012. *Rethinking Multiple Exclusion Homelessness: Implications for Workforce Development and Interprofessional Practice*. Available at: http://www.kcl.ac.uk/sspp/policyinstitute/scwru/pubs/2011/cornesetal2011homelessnesssummary.pdf.

Costello, B., Wachtel, J. & Wachtel, T., 2010. *Restorative Circles in Schools: Building Community and Enhancing Learning*. International Institute for Restorative Practices.

Costin, L.B., 1983. Edith Abbott and the Chicago influence on social work education. *Social Service Review*, *57*(1), pp. 94–111.

Coulshed, V. & Orme, J., 2012. *Social Work Practice*. Palgrave McMillan.

Courtney, K., 2017. Labour Manifesto. National Education Union, NUT Section {online}. Available at: https://www.teachers.org.uk/news-events/press-releases-england/labour-manifesto.

Crane, M., Warnes, A. & Fu, R., 2006. Developing homelessness prevention practice: combining research evidence and professional knowledge. *Health and Social Care in the Community*, *14*(2), pp. 156–166.

Cunningham, J. & Cunningham, S., 2014. *Sociology and Social Work*. Learning Matters.

Curry, N., Mundle, C., Sheil, F. & Weaks, L., 2011. *The Voluntary and Community Sector in Health Implications of the Proposed NHS Reforms*. The Kings Fund.

Cutrona, C.E., 1996. *Social Support in Couples: Marriage as a Resource in Times of Stress* (Vol. 13). Sage Publications.

Cutrona, C.E., 2000. Social support principles for strengthening families. *Family Support: Direction from Diversity*, pp. 103–122.

Daly, M., 2013. Parenting support policies in Europe. *Families, Relationships and Societies*, *2*(2), pp. 159–174.

Daly, M., Bruckhauf, Z., Byrne, J., Pecnik, N., Samms-Vaughan, M., Bray, R. & Margaria, A., 2015. *Family and Parenting Support: Policy and Provision in a Global Context* (No. innins770).

Daniel, B., Wassell, S. & Gilligan, R., 2011. *Child Development for Child Care and Protection Workers*. Jessica Kingsley Publishers.

Davies, C. & Ward, H., 2011. *Safeguarding Children Across Services: Messages from Research*. Jessica Kingsley Publishers.

Davies, K., & Jones, R., eds., 2015. *Skills for Social Work Practice*. Palgrave Macmillan.

Davies, L. & Duckett, N., 2016. *Proactive Child Protection and Social Work*. Learning Matters.

Davies, L. & Lebloch, E.K., 2013. *Communicating with Children and Their Families: Responding to Need and Protection*. McGraw-Hill Education.

Davis, J.E., Davis, J.M. & Smith, M., 2012. *Working in Multi-Professional Contexts: A Practical Guide for Professionals in Children's Services*. Sage.

Dearden, C. & Becker, S., 2004. *Young Carers in the UK: The 2004 Report*. London: Carers UK.

Department for Education and Skills, 2003. *Every Child Matters*. London: TSO.

Department for Communities and Local Government. England and Wales Citizenship Survey, 2007. Available at: www.communities.gov.uk.

Department of Health, 1995. *Child Protection: Messages from Research*. London: HMSO

Department of Health, 2000. *Assessing Children in Need and their Families: Practice Guidance*. London: The Stationery Office.

Department of Health, 2010. *Living Well with Dementia: A National Dementia Strategy*. London: HM Government.

Department of Health and Social Care, 2017. *A Framework for Mental Health Research*. London: HMSO.

Department of Health, Home Office, 2000. *Framework for the Assessment of Children in Need and Their Families*. London: The stationary office.

Devaney, C. & Dolan, P., 2017. Voice and meaning: The wisdom of family support veterans. *Child & Family Social Work, 22*(S3), pp. 10–20.

Devaney, J., 2008. Chronic child abuse and domestic violence: Children and families with long-term and complex needs. *Child & Family Social Work, 13*(4), pp. 443–453.

Devon's Multi Agency Safeguarding Hub (MASH). Available at: http://www.c4eo. org.uk/local-practice/emerging-practice-examples/devon%e2%80%99s-multi-agency-safeguarding-hub-(mash).aspx.

DfE, 2012. *Child Abuse Linked to Faith or Belief, National Action Plan 2012*. Department for Education.

DfE, 2013. *Working Together to Safeguard Children*. Department for Education.

DfE, 2015. *Working Together to Safeguard Children*. Department for Education.

DfE, 2018. *Working Together to Safeguard Children*. Department for Education.

Disability Rights UK, 2016. *The 'Affordable Papers': Contributions to an Economy That Includes Disabled People*. Available at: https://www.disabilityrightsuk. org/sites/default/files/pdf/AffordablePapers.pdf.

Dolan, P. 2006. Assessment, intervention & self appraisal tools for family support. In Dolan, P., Canavan J. & Pinkerton, J., eds., *Family Support as Reflective Practice* (pp. 197–210). London: Jessica Kingsley.

Dolan, P., 2008. Prospective possibilities for building resilience in children, their families and communities. *Child Care in Practice, 14*(1), pp. 83–91.

Dolan, P. & Brady, B., 2011. *A Guide to Youth Mentoring: Providing Effective Social Support*. Jessica Kingsley Publishers.

Dolan, P. & Frost, N., eds., 2017. *The Routledge Handbook of Global Child Welfare*. Taylor & Francis.

Dolan, P., Pinkerton, J. & Canavan, J., 2006. *Family Support as Reflective Practice*. Jessica Kingsley Publishers.

Dolan, P., Shannon, M. & Smyth, B., 2017. Family support in practice: Voices from the field. *European Journal of Social Work, 21*(5), pp. 737–749.

Dolan, P., Smith, B., Smith, M. & Davis, J., 2015. Family support and child welfare in Ireland: Capacities and possibilities. In Vincent, S., ed., *Early Intervention: Supporting and Strengthening Families*. Dunedin Academic Press.

DuBois, D.L. & Karcher, M.J., eds., 2013. *Handbook of Youth Mentoring*. Sage Publications.

Dunst, C. K., 2008. Revisiting, 'rethinking early intervention'. In Feldman, M.A., ed., *Early Intervention: The Essential Readings* (Vol. 6). John Wiley & Sons.

Dwyer, P., Bowpitt, G., Sundin, E. & Weinstein, M., 2015. Rights, responsibilities and refusals: Homelessness policy and the exclusion of single homeless people with complex needs. *Critical Social Policy 35*(1), pp. 3–23.

Dwyer, P. & Wright, S., 2014. Universal credit, ubiquitous conditionality and its implications for social citizenship. *Journal of Poverty and Social Justice, 22*(1), pp. 27–35.

Easton, C., Gee, G., Durbin, B. & Teeman, D., 2011. Early intervention, using the CAF process, and its cost effectiveness. *National Foundation for Educational Research*.

Edwards, A., 2004. The new multi-agency working: Collaborating to prevent the social exclusion of children and families. *Journal of Integrated Care, 12*(5), pp. 3–9.

Edwards, M., 2015. *Global Childhoods*. Critical Publishing.

Edwards, R., Gillies, V. & Horsley, N., 2016. Early intervention and evidence-based policy and practice: Framing and taming. *Social Policy and Society, 15*(1), pp. 1–10.

Edwards, R., & Gillies, V. 2012. Farewell to family? Notes on an argument for retaining the concept. *Families, Relationships and Societies, 1*(1), pp. 63–69.

Edwards, R., Gillies, V. & Horsley, N., 2015. Brain science and early years policy: Hopeful ethos or 'cruel optimism'? *Critical Social Policy, 35*(2), pp. 167–187.

Elmer, S., 2017. Social justice in local government. In Mealey, A.M., Jarvis, P., Doherty, J. & Fook, J., eds., 2017. *Everyday Social Justice and Citizenship: Perspectives for the 21st Century*. Routledge.

Engle, P.L., Black, M.M., Behrman, J.R., De Mello, M.C., Gertler, P.J., Kapiriri, L., Martorell, R., Young, M.E. & International Child Development Steering Group, 2007. Strategies to avoid the loss of developmental potential in more than 200 million children in the developing world. *The Lancet, 369*(9557), pp. 229–242.

Esping-Andersen, G., 1990. 4 The three political economies of the welfare state. *International Journal of Sociology, 20*(3), pp. 92–123.

Esping-Andersen, G., 2008. Childhood investments and skill formation. *International Tax and Public Finance, 15*(1), pp. 19–44.

Evangelista, F. & Jones, 2013. *Mean Streets. A European Report on Criminalising Homelessness in Europe*. Available at: http://www.housingrightswatch.org/sites/default/files/Mean%20Streets%20-%20Full.pdf.

Evans, C., 2014. Physical disabilities. In Teater, B., ed., *Contemporary Social Work Practice: A Handbook for Students*. McGraw-Hill Education.

Every Child Matters, 2003. HM Treasury. Available at: https://www.gov.uk/government/publications/every-child-matters.

'*Families at Risk' Review*, 2008. Cabinet Office. Social Exclusion Task Force.

Families First Research Review: Integrated Processes & Models of Delivery, 2011. Institute of Public Care. *Family Rights Group*. Website, Available at: http://www.frg.org.uk.

Family Drug and Alcohol Court. Available at: http://fdac.org.uk/.

Family Rights Group, *Fathers Matter Action Research Projects*, Family Valued, Leeds. Available at: http://www.leeds.gov.uk/residents/Pages/family-valued.aspx.

Farrington, D.P., 2007. Childhood risk factors and risk-focused prevention. *The Oxford Handbook of Criminology, 4*, pp. 602–640.

Feantsa. 2008. Website, Available at: www.feantsa.org.

Featherstone, B., 2003. *Family Life and Family Support: A Feminist Analysis*. Palgrave Macmillan.

Featherstone, B., 2005. Rethinking family support in the current policy context. *British Journal of Social Work, 36*(1), pp. 5–19.

Featherstone, B., Morris, K., White, S. & White, S., 2014. *Re-imagining Child Protection: Towards Humane Social Work with Families*. Policy Press.

Feeney, B.C. & Collins, N.L., 2015. A new look at social support: A theoretical perspective on thriving through relationships. *Personality and Social Psychology Review, 19*(2), pp. 113–147.

Ferguson, H., 2011. *Child Protection Practice*. Palgrave Macmillan.

Fisher-Borne, M., Cain, J.M. & Martin, S.L., 2015. From mastery to accountability: Cultural humility as an alternative to cultural competence. *Social Work Education, 34*(2), pp. 165–181.

Fitzpatrick, S. & Pleace, N., 2012. The statutory homelessness system in England: A fair and effective rights-based model?. *Housing Studies, 27*(2), pp. 232–251.

Fitzpatrick, S. & Watts, B., 2010. 'The right to housing' for homeless people. In E. O'Sullivan, V. Busch Geertsema, D. Quilgars, & N. Pleace (Eds.), Homelessness Research in Europe (pp. 105–122). Brussels:FEANTSA.

Fitzsimons, P., & William Teager, W., 2018. The cost of Late Intervention in Northern Ireland. *Early Intervention Foundation*. Available at: http://www.eif.org.uk/.

Fives, A., Kennan, D., Canavan, J., Brady, B. & Cairns, D., 2010. Study of young carers in the Irish population. *The National Children's Strategy Research Services*.

Flint, J., Batty, E., Parr, S., Platts-Fowler, D., Nixon, J., & Sanderson, D. 2011. *Evaluation of Intensive Intervention Projects*. London: Department for Education.

Flying Start. Welsh Government, Available at: http://gov.wales/topics/people-and-communities/people/children-and-young-people/parenting-support-guidance/help/flyingstart/?lang=en.

Focus Ireland. Website, Available at: www.focusireland.ie.

Foley, P., 2011. Public policy, children and young people. In O'Dell, L. & Leverett, S., eds., 2010. *Working with Children and Young People: Co-constructing Practice*. Palgrave Macmillan.

Forrester, D., Kershaw, S., Moss, H. & Hughes, L., 2008. Communication skills in child protection: How do social workers talk to parents? *Child & Family Social Work, 13*(1), pp. 41–51.

Forrester, D., Westlake, D. & Glynn, G., 2012. Parental resistance and social worker skills: Towards a theory of motivational social work. *Child & Family Social Work, 17*(2), pp. 118–129.

Fox Harding, L., 1991. *Perspectives in Child Care Policy*. London: Longman.

Frost, N., 2005. *Professionalism, Partnership and Joined-Up Thinking: A Research Review of Front-line Working with Children and Families*. Research in Practice.

Frost, N., 2014. Interagency working with children and families: What works and what makes a difference? In Foley, P. & Rixon, A., eds., *Changing Children's Services: Working and Learning Together*, p. 143. Policy Press.

Frost, N. & Dolan, P., 2012. The theoretical foundations of family support work. In Davies, M.B., ed., 2012. *Social Work with Children and Families*. Palgrave Macmillan.

Frost, N. & Robinson, M., 2007. Joining up children's services: Safeguarding children in multi-disciplinary teams. *Child Abuse Review, 16*(3), pp. 184–199.

Frost, N., Abbott, S. & Race, T., 2015. *Family Support: Prevention, Early Intervention and Early Help.* John Wiley & Sons.

Galpin, D. & Bates, N., 2009. *Social Work Practice with Adults.* Learning Matters.

Garbarino, J., 1992. *Children and Families in the Social Environment.* New York: Walter de Gryuter.

Gardner, R., 2002. *Supporting Families: Child Protection in the Community.* Wiley & Sons.

Garrett, P.M., 2004. The electronic eye: Emerging surveillant practices in social work with children and families. *European Journal of Social Work, 7*(1), pp. 57–71.

Garrett, P.M., ed., 2014. *Children and Families.* Policy Press.

Gasper, M., 2010. *Multi-agency Working in the Early Years: Challenges and Opportunities.* Sage Publications.

Geens, N., Roets, G. & Vandenbroeck, M., 2017. Parents' perspectives of social support and social cohesion in urban contexts of diversity. *European Journal of Social Work,* pp. 1–12. Available at: https://doi.org/10.1080/13691457.201 7.1366426g.

Ghate, D. & Hazel, N., 2002. *Parenting in poor environments: Stress, support and coping.* Jessica Kingsley Publishers.

Giardiello, P., 2013. *Pioneers in Early Childhood Education: The Roots and Legacies of Rachel and Margaret McMillan, Maria Montessori and Susan Isaacs.* Routledge.

Gibbons, J., Thorpe, S. & Wilkinson, P., 1990. *Family Support and Prevention: Studies in Local Areas.* HM Stationery Office.

Gilbert, N., 2012. A comparative study of child welfare systems: Abstract orientations and concrete results. *Children and Youth Services Review, 34*(3), pp. 532–536.

Gilligan, R., 2000. Adversity, resilience and young people: The protective value of positive school and spare time experiences. *Children & Society, 14*(1), pp. 37–47.

Gilligan, R., 2008. Promoting resilience in young people in long-term care – The relevance of roles and relationships in the domains of recreation and work. *Journal of Social Work Practice, 22*(1), pp. 37–50.

Gilligan, R., 2012. Children, social networks and social support. In Hill, M., Head, G., Lockyer, A., Reid, B. & Taylor, R., eds., *Children's Services: Working Together.* Routledge.

Glasby, J. & Tew, J., 2015. *Mental Health Policy and Practice.* Palgrave Macmillan.

Glass, N., 1999. Sure start: The development of an early intervention programme for young children in the United Kingdom. *Children & Society, 13*(4), pp. 257–264.

Glover, J., 2009. Bouncing back: How can resilience be promoted in vulnerable children and young people. *Barnardo's Website.* Gloucestershire Council. Available at: http://www.gloucestershire.gov.uk/health-and-social-care/ children-young-people-and-families/restorative-practice-in-gloucestershire/.

Gohir, S., 2013. Unheard voices: The sexual exploitation of Asian girls and young women. *Birmingham: Muslim Women's Network UK.*

Golightley, M., 2011. *Social Work and Mental Health.* Learning Matters.

Golightley, M. & Goemans, R., 2017. *Social Work and Mental Health*. Learning Matters.

Gray, M., 2011. Back to basics: A critique of the strengths perspective in social work. *Families in Society: The Journal of Contemporary Social Services, 92*(1), pp. 5–11.

Gray, M., 2013. The swing to early intervention and prevention and its implications for social work. *British Journal of Social Work, 44*(7), pp. 1750–1769.

Green, L. & Clarke, K., 2016. *Social Policy for Social Work: Placing Social Work in Its Wider Context*. John Wiley & Sons.

Grembowski, D., Patrick, D., Diehr, P., Durham, M., Beresford, S., Kay, E. & Hecht, J., 1993. Self-efficacy and health behavior among older adults. *Journal of Health and Social Behavior, 34*(2), pp. 89–104.

Grzymala-Kazlowska, A., 2017. From connecting to social anchoring: Adaptation and 'settlement' of polish migrants in the UK. *Journal of Ethnic and Migration Studies, 44*(2), pp. 1–18.

Hackworth, J., 2010. Faith, welfare, and the city: The mobilization of religious organizations for neoliberal ends. *Urban Geography, 31*(6), pp. 750–773.

Hall, B., 2012. Reflective social work practice with older people: The professional and the organization. In Hall, B., ed., *Social Work With Older People: Approaches To Person-centred Practice*, p. 7

Hall, J., Eisenstadt, N., Sylva, K., Smith, T., Sammons, P., Smith, G., Evangelou, M., Goff, J., Tanner, E., Agur, M. & Hussey, D., 2015. A review of the services offered by English Sure Start Children's Centres in 2011 and 2012. *Oxford Review of Education, 41*(1), pp. 89–104.

Hall, S., Leary, K. & Greevy, H., 2014. *Public Attitudes Towards Poverty*. Joseph Rowntree Foundation. Available at: https://www.jrf.org.uk/report/public-attitudes-towards-poverty.

Hardiker, P., Exton, K. & Barker, M., 1991. *Policies and Practices in Preventive Child Care*. Avebury.

Harding, L.F., 1996. The quest for 'family policy'. In Harding, L.F. & Campling, J., eds., *Family, State and Social Policy* (pp. 204–227). Basingstoke: Macmillan Education UK.

Hatton, K., 2013. Social Pedagogy in the UK. *Theory and Practice*. London: Russell House Publishing.

Hawkins, R.L. & Maurer, K., 2011. Unravelling Social Capital: Disentangling a Concept for Social Work. *British Journal of Social Work, 42*(2), pp. 353–370.

Health Equity Evidence Review 2: September 2014. *Local Action on Health Inequalities: Building Children and Young People's Resilience in Schools*. Public Health England.

Healy, T. & Côté, S., 2001. *The Well-Being of Nations: The Role of Human and Social Capital. Education and Skills*. Organisation for Economic Cooperation and Development, 2 rue Andre Pascal, F-75775 Paris Cedex 16, France.

Helyer, R., 2015. *The Work-Based Learning Student Handbook*. Palgrave Macmillan.

Highscope. Website, Available at: https://highscope.org/home.

Hill, M., Stafford, A., Seaman, P., Ross, N. & Daniel, B., 2007. *Parenting and Resilience*. York: Joseph Rowntree Foundation.

Hill, N., 2006. Disentangling ethnicity, socioeconomic status and parenting: Interactions, influences and meaning. *Vulnerable Children and Youth Studies*, *1*(1), pp. 114–124.

HM Treasury, 2007. *Aiming High for Disabled Children: Better Support for Families Policy*. London: Stationery Office.

Holland, J., 2008. *Young People and Social Capital: What Can It Do for Us*. London: Families & Social Capital Research Group.

Holland, S., Scourfield, J., O'Neill, S.E. & Pithouse, A., 2005. Democratising the family and the state? The case of family group conferences in child welfare. *Journal of Social Policy*, *34*(1), pp. 59–77.

Holman, R., 1988. *Putting Families First: Prevention and Child Care: A Study of Prevention by Statutory and Voluntary Agencies*. Macmillan Education.

Holmes, D., Parr, S., Thoburn, J., Hayden, C., Jenkins, C., Matczak, A., Byford, I., Hall, N. & Jones, R., 2015. *Social Work with Troubled Families: A Critical Introduction*. Jessica Kingsley Publishers.

Holt, A., 2011. Constructing practice within the parenting agenda: The case of Sure Start and Parenting Orders. In O'Dell, L. & Leverett, S., eds., *Working with Children and Young People: Co-constructing Practice*. Palgrave Macmillan.

Homestart. Website, Available at: https://www.home-start.org.uk/about-us.

Howe, D., 2011. *Attachment Across the Lifecourse: A Brief Introduction*. Palgrave Macmillan.

Hudson, B., 2002. Interprofessionality in health and social care: the Achilles' heel of partnership?. *Journal of Interprofessional Care*, *16*(1), pp. 7–17.

Hudson, J. & Lowe, S., 2009. *Understanding the Policy Process: Analysing Welfare Policy and Practice*. Policy Press.

Hughes, K., Ford, K., Davies, A.R., Homolova, L. & Bellis, M.A., 2018. *Sources of Resilience and their Moderating Relationships with Harms from Adverse Childhood Experiences*. Public Health Wales NHS Trust.

Hussain, F., 2006. Cultural competence, cultural sensitivity and family support. In Dolan, P., Canavan, J. & Pinkerton, J., eds., *Family Support as Reflective Practice*. London: Jessica Kingsley

IISaM: The Leicestershire Multi Agency Information Sharing Hub (MASH) – Available at: www.informationsharing.co.uk.

IRiS Research Centre. Website, Available at: https://www.birmingham.ac.uk/research/activity/superdiversity-institute/index.aspx.

International Institute for Restorative Practices. Website, Available at: https://www.iirp.edu/.

Jack, G., 1997. An ecological approach to social work with children and families. *Child and Family Social Work*, *2*, pp. 109–120.

Jack, G. & Gill, O., 2010. The role of communities in safeguarding children and young people. *Child Abuse Review*, *19*(2), pp. 82–96.

Jack, G. & Donnellan, H., 2013. *Social Work with Children*. Palgrave.

James, A. & James, A., 2004. *Constructing Childhood: Theory, Policy and Social Practice*. Macmillan.

Jamieson, L., 2011. Understanding different kinds of family in context. In Hill, M., Head, G., Lockyer, A., Reid, B. & Taylor, R., 2013. *Children's Services: Working Together*. Routledge.

Janer, À. & Úcar, X., 2017. Analysing the dimensions of social pedagogy from an international perspective. *European Journal of Social Work, 20*(2), pp. 203–218.

Jay, A., 2014. *Independent Inquiry into Child Sexual Exploitation in Rotherham: 1997–2013*. Rotherham Metropolitan Borough Council.

Johnson, R. & Cotmore, R., 2015. *National Evaluation of the Graded Care Profile*. London: NSPCC.

Johnson, R., Smith, E. & Fisher, H., 2015. *Testing the Reliability and Validity of the Graded Care Profile Version 2 (GCP2)*. London: NSPCC.

Jones, R., Bhanbhro, S.M., Grant, R. & Hood, R., 2013. The definition and deployment of differential core professional competencies and characteristics in multiprofessional health and social care teams. *Health & Social Care in the Community, 21*(1), pp. 47–58.

Jones, R., Matczak, A., Davis, K. & Byford, I., 2015. 'Troubled families': A team around the family. In Davis, M., ed., *Social Work with Troubled Families: A Critical Introduction* (p. 124).

Jordan, B. & Drakeford, M., 2012. *Social Work and Social Policy Under Austerity*. Palgrave Macmillan.

Joseph Rowntree Foundation. Website, Available at: https://www.jrf.org.uk/.

Joslyn, E., 2015. *Resilience in Childhood: Perspectives, Promise & Practice*. Palgrave Macmillan.

Just Fair, 2014. *Protecting the Right to Housing in England: A Context of Crisis*. Available at: http://just-fair.co.uk/uploads/The_Right_to_Housing_FINAL_27.07.15_.pdf.

Keddell, E., 2014. Theorising the signs of safety approach to child protection social work: Positioning, codes and power. *Children and Youth Services Review, 47*, pp. 70–77.

Kenny, S., Taylor, M., Onyx, J. & Mayo, M., 2015. *Challenging the Third Sector: Global Prospects for Active Citizenship*. Policy Press.

Kerr, B., Gordon, J., MacDonald, C. & Stalker, K., 2005. *Effective Social Work with Older People*. Edinburgh: Scottish Executive Social Research.

Khalifa, S. & Brown, E. 2016, 'Communities tackling FGM in the UK: Best practice guide'. *The Tackling Female Genital Mutilation Initiative and Options*. London: Consultancy Services Limited.

Kirmayer, L.J., 2012. Rethinking cultural competence. *Transcultural Psychiatry, 49*(2), pp. 149–116.

Kirton, D., 2008. *Child Social Work Policy & Practice*. Sage.

Knight, K.H., Porcellato, L. & Tume, L., 2014. Out-of-school lives of physically disabled children and young people in the United Kingdom: A qualitative literature review. *Journal of Child Health Care, 18*(3), pp. 275–285.

Laban, C.J., 2015. Resilience-oriented treatment of traumatised asylum seekers and refugees. In Schouler-Ocak, M., ed., *Trauma and Migration: Cultural Factors in the Diagnosis and Treatment of Traumatised Immigrants* (pp. 191–208). Springer.

Laming, L. H., 2003. *The Victoria Climbie Inquiry: Report of an Inquiry by Lord Laming*. London: The Stationery Office.

Laming, L. H. 2009 *The Protection of Children in England: A Progress Report*. London: The Stationery Office.

Lansdown, G., 2011. Children's Welfare and Children's Rights. In O'Dell, L. & Leverett, S., eds., *Working with Children and Young People: Co-constructing Practice*. Palgrave Macmillan.

Larson, C.E. & LaFasto, F.M., eds., 2003. *Teamwork*. Sage.

Leadbetter, J., Daniels, H., Edwards, A., Martin, D., Middleton, D., Popova, A., Warmington, P., Apostolov, A. & Brown, S., 2007. Professional learning within multi-agency children's services: researching into practice. *Educational Research, 49*(1), pp. 83–98.

Lesson plans and guidance for promoting Gypsy Roma Traveller awareness in the primary classroom. Available at: http://www.histories.info/lesson-plans-and-guidance-for-promoting-gypsy-roma-traveller-a.html.

Leverett, S., 2014. Parenting, practice and politics. In Foley, P. & Rixon, A., eds., *Changing Children's Services: Working and Learning Together*. Policy Press.

Levin, J., 2013. *Blurring the Boundaries: The Declining Significance of Age*. Routledge.

Levitas, R. 2014 *'Troubled Families' in a Spin*. Available at: http://www.poverty.ac.uk/sites/default/files/attachments/Troubled%20Families%20in%20a%20Spin.pdf.

Lewis, J. & Surender, R. eds., 2004. *Welfare State Change: Towards a Third Way?*. Oxford: Oxford University Press.

Lietz, C.A., 2011. Theoretical adherence to family centered practice: Are strengths-based principles illustrated in families' descriptions of child welfare services? *Children and Youth Services Review, 33*(6), pp. 888–893.

Lister, R., 2004. The third way's social investment state. *Welfare State Change. Towards a Third Way*, pp. 157–181.

Lister, R. 2006. An agenda for children: Investing in the future or promoting well-being in the present? In Lewis, J., ed., *Children, Changing Families and Welfare States*. Cheltenham: Edward Elgar.

Lonne, B., Parton, N., Thomson, J. & Harries, M., 2008. *Reforming Child Protection*. Routledge.

Lwin, K., Versanov, A., Cheung, C., Goodman, D., & Andrews, N. 2014. The use of mapping in child welfare investigations. A strengths based hybrid intervention. *Child Care in Practice, 20*(1), pp. 81–97.

Lymbery, M., 2005. *Social Work with Older People*. Sage.

Lymbery, M. & Postle, K., 2010. Social work in the context of adult social care in England and the resultant implications for social work education. *British Journal of Social Work, 40*(8), pp. 2502–2522.

Macvarish, J., Lee, E. & Lowe, P., 2015. Neuroscience and family policy: What becomes of the parent? *Critical Social Policy, 35*(2), pp. 248–269.

Maeseele, T., Roose, R., Bouverne-De Bie, M. & Roets, G., 2013. From vagrancy to homelessness: The value of a welfare approach to homelessness. *British Journal of Social Work, 44*(7), pp. 1717–1734.

Malin, N., Tunmore, J. & Wilcock, A., 2014. How far does a whole family approach make a difference. *Social Work and Social Sciences Review, 17*(2), pp. 63–92.

Marsh, P. & Crow, G., 1998. *Family Group Conferences in Child Welfare*. Blackwell Science.

Martin, D., 2014. Mental health. In Teater, B., ed., *Contemporary Social Work Practice: A Handbook for Students*. McGraw-Hill Education.

Martin, G., Gardner, M. & Brooks Gunn, J., 2012. The mediated and moderated effects of family support on child maltreatment. *Journal of Family Studies, 33*(7), pp. 920–941.

Mason, P., Ferguson, H., Morris, K., Munton, T. & Sen, R., 2017. *Leeds Family Valued Evaluation Report.* Children's Social Care Innovation Programme Evaluation Report 4: Department for Education.

Matthews, P. & Besemer, K., 2015. Social networks, social capital and poverty: Panacea or placebo? *Journal of Poverty and Social Justice, 23*(3), pp. 189–201.

Mayall, B., 2015. The sociology of childhood and children's rights. In Vandenhole, W., Desmet, E., Reynaert, D. & Lembrechts, S., eds., *Routledge International Handbook of Children's Rights Studies*, pp. 147–163. Routledge.

McAndrew, S., Warne, T., Fallon, D. & Moran, P., 2012. Young, gifted, and caring: A project narrative of young carers, their mental health, and getting them involved in education, research and practice. *International Journal of Mental Health Nursing, 21*(1), pp. 12–19.

McAuley, C., Pecora, P. & Rose, W., eds., 2006. *Enhancing the Well-Being of Children and Families through Effective Interventions. International Evidence for Practice* (pp. 46–57). London: Jessica Kingsley.

McCormack, J., 2012. Family support work in practice. In Davies, M.B., ed., *Social Work with Children and Families.* Palgrave Macmillan.

McGrath, B., Brennan, M.A., Dolan, P. & Barnett, R., 2009. Adolescent well-being and supporting contexts: A comparison of adolescents in Ireland and Florida. *Journal of Community & Applied Social Psychology, 19*(4), pp. 299–320.

McKeown, K. 2003. *Family Well-being, What Makes a Difference.* Dublin: Stationery Office.

McKeown, K., 2013 *Using Evidence to Develop Services for Children and Families.* Administration, Volume 61, No 1, April 2013.

McLaughlin, H., 2011. *Understanding Social Work Research.* Sage.

McLaughlin, H. 2013 Motherhood, apple pie and interprofessional practice. *Social Work Education: The International Journal, 32*(7), pp. 956–963.

McLeod, A., 2008. *Listening to Children: A Practitioner's Guide.* Jessica Kingsley Publishers.

Meissner, F. & Vertovec, S., 2015. Comparing super-diversity. *Ethnic and Racial Studies, 38*(4), pp. 541–555.

Mels, C., Derluyn, I. & Broekaert, E., 2008. Social support in unaccompanied asylum-seeking boys: A case study. *Child: Care, Health and Development, 34*(6), pp. 757–762.

Mental Health Foundation. Website, Available at: https://www.mentalhealth.org.uk/publications/health-inequalities-manifesto-2018.

Mešl, N. & Kodele, T. 2016. *Co-creating Processes of Help: Collaboration with Families in the Community.* Ljubljana: Faculty of Social Work.

Miller, S., 2010. *Supporting Parents: Improving Outcomes for Children, Families and Communities.* McGraw-Hill Education.

Miller, W.R. & Rollnick, S., 2012. *Motivational Interviewing: Helping People Change.* Guilford Press.

Milne, A., Sullivan, M.P., Tanner, D., Richards, S., Ray, M., Lloyd, L., Beech, C. & Phillips, J., 2014. Social work with older people: A vision for the future. *London, The College of Social Work.* Available at: http://cdn. basw. co. uk/upload/basw_103616-1.pdf.

Milner, J., Myers, S. & O'Byrne, P., 2015. *Assessment in Social Work*. Palgrave Macmillan.

Molly, D., Barton, S., & Brims, L., 2017. *Improving the Effectiveness of the Child Protection System Overview*. London: Early Intervention Foundation.

Morabito, C., Vandenbroeck, M. & Roose, R., 2013. 'The greatest of equalisers': A critical review of international organisations' views on early childhood care and education. *Journal of Social Policy*, *42*(3), pp. 451–467.

Moran, P. & Ghate, D., 2005. The effectiveness of parenting support. *Children & Society*, *19*(4), pp. 329–336.

Morgan, D., 2011. *Rethinking Family Practices*. Springer.

Morris, K., 2011. Thinking family? The complexities for family engagement in care and protection. *British Journal of Social Work*, *42*(5), pp. 906–920.

Morris, K., 2012. Family support: policies for practice. In Davies, M.B., ed., 2012. *Social work with children and families*. Macmillan International Higher Education.

Morris, K., 2013. Troubled families: Vulnerable families' experiences of multiple service use. *Child & Family Social Work*, *18*(2), pp. 198–206.

Morris, K. & Tunnard, J., eds., 1996. *Family Group Conferences: Messages from UK Practice and Research*. London: Family Rights Group.

Moss, P. & Petrie, P., 2005. *From Children's Services to Children's Spaces: Public Policy, Children and Childhood*. Routledge.

Munro, E., 2011. *The Munro Review of Child Protection: Interim Report, The Child's Journey* (Vol. 8062). The Stationery Office.

Munro, E., 2011. *The Munro Review of Child Protection: Final Report, a Child-Centred System* (Vol. 8062). The Stationery Office.

Munro, Turnell & Murphy, Child Protection Consulting. Website, Available at: http://www.munroturnellmurphy.com/.

Murray, L., & Barnes, M. 2010. Have families been rethought? Ethic of care, family and 'whole family' approaches. *Social Policy and Society*, *9*(04), pp. 533–544.

National Institute for Clinical Excellence. Website, Available at: www.nice.org.uk.

National Youth Agency and Network of Regional Youth Work Units, 2014. *Youth Services in England: Changes and Trends in the Provision of Services*. Available at: www.nya.org.uk/resource/youth-services-englandchanges-trends-service-provision/.

Ndhlovu, F., 2016. A decolonial critique of diaspora identity theories and the notion of superdiversity. *Diaspora Studies*, *9*(1), pp. 28–40.

NESTAC. Website, Available at: http://www.nestac.org/Nestac/ourprojects.html.

NHS & Community Care Act, 1990. London: The Stationary Office.

Ní Raghallaigh, M. & Gilligan, R., 2010. Active survival in the lives of unaccompanied minors: Coping strategies, resilience, and the relevance of religion. *Child & Family Social Work*, *15*(2), pp. 226–237.

Nurullah, A.S., 2012. Received and provided social support: A review of current evidence and future directions. *American Journal of Health Studies*, *27*, p. 3.

O'Dell, L., 2011. Constructions of normative families. In O'Dell, L. & Leverett, S., eds., *Working with Children and Young People: Co-constructing Practice*. Palgrave Macmillan.

Office for National Statistics. Website, Available at: www.ONS.gov.uk.

Ofsted 2003, in Every Traveller Child Matters Too: A response to *Every Child Matters* by the Romany Gypsy community in Devon. Available at: european-dialogue.org/pdfs/EveryChild_booklet.pdf.

Oliver, K.G., Collin, P., Burns, J. & Nicholas, J., 2006. Building resilience in young people through meaningful participation. *Australian e-Journal for the Advancement of Mental Health, 5*(1), pp. 34–40.

Oliver, M., 2013. The social model of disability: thirty years on. In *Disability & Society, 28*(7), pp. 1024–1026.

Oliver, C. & Charles, G., 2015. Enacting firm, fair and friendly practice: A model for strengths-based child protection relationships? *The British Journal of Social Work, 46*(4), pp. 1009–1026.

O'Neill, A., 2017. *Hate Crime, England and Wales, 2016/17 Statistical Bulletin 17/17.* Home Office.

O'Reilly, L. & Dolan, P., 2016. The voice of the child in social work assessments: Age-appropriate communication with children. *The British Journal of Social Work, 46*(5), pp. 1191–1207.

O'Sullivan, E. & Evangelista, F., 2013. *Penalisation of Homelessness and Prison – Prison and Inequality.* Available at: http://www.housingrightswatch.org/sites/default/files/Mean%20Streets%20-%20Full.pdf.

O'Sullivan, T., 2012. Parenting and family relationships in context. In Adams, R., ed., 2011. *Working with Children and Families: Knowledge and Contexts for Practice.* Palgrave Macmillan.

Outcomes Star. Website, Available at: http://www.outcomesstar.org.uk/.

Parr, S. 2009. Family intervention projects: A site of social work practice. *British Journal of Social Work, 39*(7), pp. 1256–1273.

Parr, S., 2015. Conceptualising 'the relationship' in intensive key worker support as a therapeutic medium. *Journal of Social Work Practice, 30*(1), pp. 25–42.

Parton, N., 2005. *Safeguarding Childhood.* London: Palgrave Macmillan.

Parton, N., 2014. *The Politics of Child Protection: Contemporary Developments and Future Directions.* Palgrave Macmillan.

Pavee Point Traveller and Roma centre. Website, Available at: http://www.paveepoint.ie/.

Payne, M., 2014. *Modern Social Work Theory.* Palgrave Macmillan.

Pearce, C., 2011. *A Short Introduction to Promoting Resilience in Children.* Jessica Kingsley Publishers.

Pennell, J. & Burford, G., 2000. Family group decision making: Protecting children and women. *Child Welfare, 79*(2), p. 131.

Perry, E., 2009. Working with older people: Managing risk and promoting independence. In Galpin, D. & Bates, N., eds., *Social Work Practice with Adults.* Learning Matters.

Philips, T., 2004. Chair of the commission for racial equality. Available at: http://news.bbc.co.uk/2/hi/uk_news/england/3751214.stm.

Pichot, T. & Dolan, Y.M., 2014. *Solution-Focused Brief Therapy: Its Effective Use in Agency Settings.* Routledge.

Pinney, A., 2016. Understanding the needs of disabled children with complex needs or life-limiting conditions: What can we learn from national data.

Available at: https://councilfordisabledchildren.org.uk/help-resources/resources/understanding-needs-disabled-children-complex-needs-or-life-limiting-conditions.

Pithouse, A.J. & Emlyn-Jones, R., 2015. Early intervention: A perspective from Wales. *Early Intervention: Supporting and Strengthening Families* (pp. 125–140). Dunedin Academic Press.

Pollard, K., Sellman, D. & Senior, B., 2005. The need for interprofessional working. In Barrett, G., Sellman, D. & Thomas, J., eds., *Interprofessional Working in Health and Social Care: Professional Perspectives* (pp. 7–17). New York: Palgrave Macmillan.

Prochaska, J.O., DiClemente, C.C. & Norcross, J.C., 1992. In search of how people change: Applications to addictive behaviors. *American Psychologist*, *47*(9), p. 1102.

Putnam, R.D., 1993. The prosperous community. *The American Prospect*, *4*(13), pp. 35–42.

Quinney, A., 2006. *Collaborative Social Work Practice*. Exeter: Learning Matters.

Quinney, A. & Hafford-Letchfield, T., 2012. *Interprofessional Social Work: Effective Collaborative Approaches*. Learning Matters.

Race, T. & O'Keefe, R., 2017. *Child-Centred Practice: A Handbook for Social Work*. Macmillan International Higher Education.

Rapp, C.A., Saleebey, D. & Sullivan, W.P., 2006. The future of strengths-based social work. *Advances in Social Work: Special Issue on the Futures of Social Work*, *6*(1), pp. 79–90.

Realigning Children's Services, Scottish Government. Available at: http://www.gov.scot/Topics/People/Young-People/realigning-childrens-services.

Reder, P. & Duncan, S., 2004. From Colwell to Climbie: Inquiring into fatal child abuse. In *The Age of the Inquiry: Learning and Blaming in Health and Social Care* (pp. 92–115). London: Routledge.

Refugee Action. Website, Available at: www.refugee-action.org.uk.

Refugee Survival Trust. Website, Available at: www.rst.org.uk/.

Ridge, T., 2002. *Childhood Poverty and Social Exclusion: From a Child's Perspective*. Policy Press.

Ridge, T., 2011. The everyday costs of poverty in childhood: A review of qualitative research exploring the lives and experiences of low-income children in the UK. *Children & Society*, *25*(1), pp. 73–84.

Rixon, A., 2011. Wellbeing and the ecology of children's lives. In O'Dell, L. & Leverett, S., eds., 2010. *Working with Children and Young People: Co-constructing Practice*. Palgrave Macmillan.

Robinson, L., 2007. *Cross-cultural Child Development for Social Workers: An Introduction*. Palgrave Macmillan.

Robson, K., Tooby, A. & Duschinsky, R., 2015. Love barrow families: A case study of transforming public services. *Early Intervention: Supporting and Strengthening Families* (pp. 125–140). Dunedin Academic Press.

Roets, G., Roose, R., Schiettecat, T. & Vandenbroeck, M., 2014. Reconstructing the foundations of joined-up working: From organisational reform towards a joint engagement of child and family services. *British Journal of Social Work*, *46*(2), pp. 306–322.

Rogowski, S., 2011. Managers, managerialism and social work with children and families: The deformation of a profession? *Practice, 23*(3), pp. 157–167.

Rohe, W.M., 2004. Building social capital through community development. *Journal of the American Planning Association, 70*(2), pp. 158–164.

Roose, R., Roets, G. & Schiettecat, T., 2014. Implementing a strengths perspective in child welfare and protection: A challenge not to be taken lightly. *European Journal of Social Work, 17*(1), pp. 3–17.

Rose, W., 2015. The policy context in Scotland. *Early Intervention: Supporting and Strengthening Families* (pp. 125–140). Dunedin Academic Press.

Rostgaard, T., 2004. Family support policy in central and eastern Europe – A decade and a half of transition. *Early Childhood and Family Policy Series, 8*, pp. 1–37.

Ruch, G., Turney, D. & Ward, A., 2010. *Relationship-Based Practice: Getting to the Heart of Practice*. London: Jessica Kingsley.

Rutter, M., 1985. Resilience in the face of adversity. Protective factors and resistance to psychiatric disorder. *The British Journal of Psychiatry, 147*(6), pp. 598–611.

Saint-Jacques, M.C., Turcotte, D. & Pouliot, E., 2009. Adopting a strengths perspective in social work practice with families in difficulty: From theory to practice. *Families in Society: The Journal of Contemporary Social Services, 90*(4), pp. 454–461.

Saleeby, D. 1992. *The Strengths Perspective in Social Work Practice*. New York: Longman.

Saleeby, D. 2006. *The Strengths Perspective in Social Work Practice* (4th edn). New York: Pearson/Allyn and Bacon.

Samantrai, K., 2004. *Culturally Competent Public Child Welfare Practice*. Brooks/Cole Publishing Company.

Sanders, J.M., 2002. Ethnic boundaries and identity in plural societies. *Annual Review of Sociology, 28*(1), pp. 327–357.

Sawyer, E. & Burton, S., 2016. *A Practical Guide to Early Intervention and Family Support: Assessing Needs and Building Resilience in Families Affected by Parental Mental Health Problems or Substance Misuse*. Jessica Kingsley Publishers.

Schouler-Ocak, M., Wintrob, R., Moussaoui, D., Villasenor Bayardo, S.J., Zhao, X.D. & Kastrup, M.C., 2016. Background paper on the needs of migrant, refugee and asylum seeker patients around the globe. *International Journal of Culture and Mental Health, 9*(3), pp. 216–232.

Schweinhart, L.J., 2005. *Lifetime Effects: The High/Scope Perry Preschool Study through Age 40* (No. 14). High/Scope Foundation.

Scottish Public Health. Website, Available at: www.healthscotland.com.

Seligman, M. & Darling, R.B., 2017. *Ordinary Families, Special Children: A Systems Approach to Childhood Disability*. Guilford Publications.

Shaw, J. & Frost, N., 2013. *Young People and the Care Experience: Research, Policy and Practice*. Routledge.

Shemmings, D. & Shemmings, Y., 2014. *Assessing Disorganized Attachment Behaviour in Children: An Evidence-Based Model for Understanding and Supporting Families*. Jessica Kingsley Publishers.

Shennan, G., 2014. *Solution-focused Practice: Effective Communication to Facilitate Change*. Palgrave Macmillan.

Sheppard, M., 2002. Depressed mothers' experience of partnership in child and family care. *British Journal of Social Work, 32*(1), pp. 93–112.

Sheppard, M., 2007. High thresholds and prevention in children's services: The impact of mothers' coping strategies on outcome of child and parenting problems – six month follow-up. *British Journal of Social Work, 39*(1), pp. 46–63.

Sheppard, M., 2012. Preventive orientations in children's centres: A study of centre managers. *British Journal of Social Work, 42*(2), pp. 265–282.

Sidebotham, P., Brandon, M., Bailey, S., Belderson, P., Garstang, J., Harrison, E., Retzer, A. & Sorensen, P., 2016. Pathways to harm, pathways to protection: a triennial analysis of serious case reviews 2011–2014.

Singh, G. & Cowden, S., 2011. Multiculturalism's new fault lines: Religious fundamentalisms and public policy. *Critical Social Policy, 31*(3), pp. 343–364.

Singh, S., 2013. Anti-racist social work education. *Anti-racism in Social Work Practice, 1*, p. 25.

Skills for Care. Website, Available at: www.skillsforcare.org.uk.

Sloper, P., 1999. Models of service support for parents of disabled children. What do we know? What do we need to know? *Child: Care, Health and Development, 25*(2), pp. 85–99.

Sloper, P., Greco, V., Beecham, J. & Webb, R., 2006. Key worker services for disabled children: What characteristics of services lead to better outcomes for children and families? *Child: Care, Health and Development, 32*(2), pp. 147–157.

Smeaton, D., 2009. *The Social Support Needs of the 80 Plus.* London: The Policy Studies Institute.

Smart, C., 2007. *Personal Life.* Polity.

Smethurst, C., 2017. 'Class inequality and social work: 'We're all in this together?'. In Bhatti-Sinclair, K. & Colin Smethurst, C., eds., *Diversity, Difference and Dilemmas: Analysing Concepts and Developing Skills.* Open University.

Smyth, B., Shannon, M. & Dolan, P., 2015. Transcending borders: Social support and resilience, the case of separated children. *Transnational Social Review, 5*(3), pp. 274–295.

Social Services and Well-being (Wales) Act 2014. Welsh Government. Social pedagogy. Website, Available at: www.socialpegagogy.uk.com.

Sheffield City Council. Website, Available at: http://www.sheffkids.co.uk/adultssite/pages/communicrateworksheets.html.

Spence, J., 2007. Support. In Robb, M., ed., *Youth in Context: Frameworks, Settings and Encounters.* SAGE Publications Ltd.

Spicer, D., 2018. *Joint Serious Case Review Concerning Sexual Exploitation of Children and Adults with Needs for Care and Support in Newcastle-upon-Tyne.* Newcastle Safeguarding Children Board and Newcastle Safeguarding Adults Board.

Spratt, T. & Callan, J., 2004. Parents' views on social work interventions in child welfare cases. *British Journal of Social Work, 34*(2), pp. 199–224.

Stafford, A., Vincent, S., Parton, N. & Smith, C., 2011. *Child Protection Systems in the United Kingdom: A Comparative Analysis.* Jessica Kingsley Publishers.

Stalker, K., MacDonald, C., King, C., McFaul, F., Young, C. & Hawthorn, M., 2015. 'We could kid on that this is going to benefit the kids but no, this is about funding': Cutbacks in services to disabled children and young people in Scotland. *Child Care in Practice, 21*(1), pp. 6–21.

Stanley, N., Ellis, J., Farrelly, N., Hollinghurst, S., Bailey, S. & Downe, S., 2015. Preventing domestic abuse for children and young people (PEACH): a mixed knowledge scoping review. Project report. London: National Institute for Health Research.

Stanley, N. & Humphreys, C., 2017. Identifying the key components of a 'whole family' intervention for families experiencing domestic violence and abuse. *Journal of Gender-Based Violence, 1*(1), pp. 99–115.

Stein, M., 2012. *Young People Leaving Care: Supporting Pathways to Adulthood.* Jessica Kingsley Publishers.

Stevens, M., Roberts, H. & Shiell, A., 2010. Research review: Economic evidence for interventions in children's social care: Revisiting the what works for children project. *Child & Family Social Work, 15*(2), pp. 145–154.

Stevenson, J., Demack, S., Stiell, B., Abdi, M., Clarkson, S., Ghaffar, F. & Hassan, S., 2017. *The Social Mobility Challenges Faced by Young Muslims.* The Social Mobility Commission.

Stokes, J. & Schmidt, G., 2011. Race, poverty and child protection decision making. *British Journal of Social Work, 41*(6), pp. 1105–1121.

Stone, B. & Rixon, A., 2008. Towards integrated working. *Changing Children's Services: Working and Learning Together,* pp. 49–92. Bristol: Policy Press.

Sundell, K. & Vinnerljung, B., 2004. Outcomes of family group conferencing in Sweden: A 3-year follow-up. *Child Abuse & Neglect, 28*(3), pp. 267–287.

Sylvester, J., Donnell, N., Gray, S., Higgins, K. & Stalker, K., 2014. A survey of disabled children and young people's views about their quality of life. *Disability & Society, 29*(5), pp. 763–777.

Taylor, B., & Rogaly, B. 2007. 'Mrs Fairly is a Dirty, Lazy Type': Unsatisfactory households and the problem of problem families in Norwich 1942–1963. *Twentieth Century British History, 18*(4), pp. 429–452.

Taylor-Gooby, P., 2008. The new welfare state settlement in Europe. *European Societies, 10*(1), pp. 3–24.

Teater, B., 2014. *An Introduction to Applying Social Work Theories and Methods.* McGraw-Hill Education.

Tedam, P., Curran, B., Singh, S., Kennedy, S., Chukwuemeka, C. & Crofts, P., 2013. *Anti-racism in Social Work Practice.* Critical Publishing.

Tétreault, S., Blais-Michaud, S., Marier Deschênes, P., Beaupré, P., Gascon, H., Boucher, N. & Carrière, M., 2014. How to support families of children with disabilities? An exploratory study of social support services. *Child & Family Social Work, 19*(3), pp. 272–281.

The Carers Trust. Website, Available at: https://carers.org/.

The Poverty and Social Exclusion website. Website, Available at: www.poverty.ac.uk.

The Refugee Council. Website, Available at: www.refugeecouncil.org.uk.

The Runnymede Trust. Website, Available at: www.runnymedetrust.org.

Thompson, N., 2006. *Promoting Workplace Learning.* Policy Press.

Thompson, N., 2011. *Promoting Equality: Working with Diversity and Difference.* Palgrave Macmillan.

Thompson, N., 2011. The family in social context. In Adams, R., ed., *Working with Children and Families: Knowledge and Contexts for Practice.* Palgrave Macmillan.

Tinson, A., Ayrton,C., Barker, K., Born, T.B., Aldridge, H. & Kenway, P., 2016. *Monitoring Poverty and Social Exclusion 2016 (MPSE)*. Joseph Rowntree Foundation. Available at: https://www.jrf.org.uk/report/monitoring-poverty-and-social-exclusion-2016.

Tovey, W., 2007. *The Post-Qualifying Handbook for Social Workers*. Jessica Kingsley Publishers.

Trivette, C.M., Dunst, C.J. & Hamby, D.W., 2010. Influences of family-systems intervention practices on parent-child interactions and child development. *Topics in Early Childhood Special Education, 30*(1), pp. 3–19.

Tunstill, J., Aldgate, J. & Hughes, M., 2006. *Improving Children's Services Networks: Lessons from Family Centres*. Jessica Kingsley Publishers.

Turnell, A. & Edwards, S., 1999. *Signs of Safety: A Solution and Safety Oriented Approach to Child Protection Casework*. New York: Norton.

Turnell, A., Pecora, P.J., Roberts, Y.H., Caslor, M. & Koziolek, D., 2017. Signs of safety: Reorienting work with children, families and communities. In Connolly, M., ed., *Beyond the Risk Paradigm in Child Protection: Current Debates and New Directions*, p. 130. Palgrave.

Ulin, J.V., Edwards, H. & O'Brien, S., 2013. *Race and Immigration in the New Ireland*. University of Notre Dame Press.

UN Convention on the Rights of the Child (UNCRC). United Nations Convention on Refugees. Available at: http://www.unhcr.org/3b66c2aa10.pdf.

Ungar, M., 2008. Resilience across cultures. *The British Journal of Social Work, 38*(2), pp. 218–235.

Ureche, H. & Franks, M., 2007. *This is Who We Are: A Study of the Views and Identities of Roma, Gypsy and Traveller Young People in England*. The Childrens Society.

Utting, W.B., 1997. *People Like Us: The Report of the Review of the Safeguards for Children Living away from Home*. Stationery Office Books (TSO).

Van Cleemput, P., 2010. Social exclusion of Gypsies and Travellers: Health impact. *Journal of Research in Nursing, 15*(4), pp. 315–327.

Vincent, S., ed., 2015. *Early Intervention: Supporting and Strengthening Families*. Dunedin Academic Press Limited.

Vincent, S. & Petch, A., 2012. *Audit and Analysis of Significant Case Reviews*. The Scottish Government.

Vincent, S. & Petch, A., 2017. Understanding child, family, environmental and agency risk factors: Findings from an analysis of significant case reviews in Scotland. *Child & Family Social Work, 22*(2), pp. 741–750.

Wachtel, T. & McCold, P. 2000. Restorative justice in everyday life. In Braithwaite, J. & Strang, H., eds., *Restorative Justice in Civil Society* (pp. 117–125). New York: Cambridge University Press.

Walker, S., 2013. *Modern Mental Health*. Critical Publishing Ltd.

Walker, S., 2015. Family therapy and systemic practice. In Lishman, J., ed., *Handbook for Practice Learning in Social Work and Social Care: Knowledge and Theory*. Jessica Kingsley Publishers.

Wastell, D. & White, S., 2017. *Blinded by Science: The Social Implications of Epigenetics and Neuroscience*. Policy Press.

Weinstein, J., Whittington, C. & Leiba, T., 2003. *Collaboration in Social Work. Practice.* Jessica Kingsley.

Welshman, J. 1999. The social history of social work: The issue of the 'problem family', 1940–70. *British Journal of Social Work, 29*(3), pp. 457–476.

Welshman, J. 2012. 'Troubled families': The lessons of history, 1880–2012. *History and Politics.* Available at: http://www.historyandpolicy.org/policy-papers/papers/troubled-families-the-lessons-of-history-1880-2012#S1.

Wheeler, J. & Hogg, V. 2012. Signs of safety and the child protection movement. In Franklin, C., Trepper, T.S., Gingerich, W. & McCollum, E., eds., *Solution Focused Brief Therapy. A Handbook of Evidence-Based Practice.* Oxford University Press.

Whipple, E.E. & Whyte, J.D., 2009. Evaluation of a Healthy Families America (HFA) programme: A deeper understanding. *British Journal of Social Work, 40*(2), pp. 407–425.

Whitfield, D., 2015. The new health and social care economy. *Sefton MBC, Liverpool and Greater Manchester City Regions and North West Regional Economy. Bootle: European Services Strategy Unit/New Directions.* Available at: https://www.european-services-strategy.org.uk/.

Whittaker, J.K. & Garbarino, J., eds., 1983. *Social Support Networks: Informal Helping in the Human Services.* Transaction Publishers.

Whittaker, K.A., Cox, P., Thomas, N. & Cocker, K., 2014. A qualitative study of parents' experiences using family support services: Applying the concept of surface and depth. *Health & Social Care in the Community, 22*(5), pp. 479–487.

Winter, K., 2010. *Building Relationships and Communicating with Young Children: A Practical Guide for Social Workers.* Routledge.

World Health Organisation. Available at: http://www.who.int/mental_health/maternal-child/child_adolescent/en/

Wyness, M.G., 2012. *Sociology of Childhood.* Oxford University Press.

Index